ISBN 978-1-330-31760-0
PIBN 10025084

English
Français
Deutsche
Italiano
Español
Português

www.forgottenbooks.com

Mythology Photography **Fiction**
Fishing Christianity **Art** Cooking
Essays Buddhism Freemasonry
Medicine **Biology** Music **Ancient
Egypt** Evolution Carpentry Physics
Dance Geology **Mathematics** Fitness
Shakespeare **Folklore** Yoga Marketing
Confidence Immortality Biographies
Poetry **Psychology** Witchcraft
Electronics Chemistry History **Law**
Accounting **Philosophy** Anthropology
Alchemy Drama Quantum Mechanics
Atheism Sexual Health **Ancient History**
Entrepreneurship Languages Sport
Paleontology Needlework Islam
Metaphysics Investment Archaeology
Parenting Statistics Criminology
Motivational

The Story of
DOCTOR JOHNSON

Being an Introduction to
BOSWELL'S *Life*

By S. C. ROBERTS, M.A.
Sometime Scholar of Pembroke College, Cambridge

CAMBRIDGE
AT THE UNIVERSITY PRESS
1919

UXORI CARISSIMAE
IN MEMORIAM
NOCTIUM BOSWELLIANARUM

PREFACE

THE object of this little book is clearly expressed on the title-page; and the title-page might be left to speak for itself, were it not for the inevitable criticism that Boswell needs no introduction. "The most discreet of cicerones" it has been said "is an intruder when we open our old favourite, and, without further magic, retire into that delicious nook of eighteenth-century society[1]."

This is from the point of view of the literary man, the "true lover" of Boswell; but the *Life* is a long and, outwardly, formidable work with which many, who might have been true lovers, have, through lack of an introduction, hardly attained even to a casual acquaintance.

The usefulness, then, of such a book as this can be tested by one question: Is a man more, or less, likely to read Boswell and to read him with enjoyment, because, as a boy, he has been told the story of Dr Johnson in simpler form?

This "simpler form" may require a little explanation.

I have not been so foolish or so sacrilegious as to attempt to paraphrase Boswell for the young; on the other hand, I have not merely strung together a series of extracts and offered them as the

[1] Sir Leslie Stephen, *Hours in a Library*.

gems of the Boswellian narrative. But, letting Boswell for the most part speak for himself—not in isolated tit-bits, but in substantial paragraphs —I have endeavoured to present Dr Johnson, in the various stages of his career and in the varied circle of his friends, in such a way as to attract

the "delicious nook"

In one or two of the chapters I have turned to the records of other friends besides Boswell— notably Mrs Thrale and Fanny Burney.

For the many imperfections that critics will discover I must plead certain limitations: my range of authorities was limited by remoteness from a large library; my space by the modest design of the book; my time by the imminence of an army medical board.

Much, indeed, is omitted, but if I shall win new readers for Boswell, I shall dare to say, like Johnson, that something likewise is performed.

S. C. R.

April 1918.

CONTENTS

ILLUSTRATIONS

The design on the cover is from one of the "copper pieces
struck at Birmingham with his [Johnson's] head impressed
on them." They passed current, as Boswell tells us, "as half-
pence there, and in the neighbouring parts of the country."

Acknowledgment is made to Messrs T. Werner Laurie Ltd
for permission to reproduce the photograph of Johnson's
house in Gough Square from Lang's *Literary London*; to
Messrs Sidgwick and Jackson Ltd for supplying the block of
the Boswell portrait; to Messrs George Routledge & Sons
Ltd for permission to reproduce the pictures facing p. 88
from Doran's *Annals of the English Stage* (ed. Lowe, 1888);
and to Messrs Emery Walker Ltd for permission to reproduce
the portrait of Garrick facing p. 92.

The Story of
DOCTOR JOHNSON

Johnson's World

O N the title-page of *The Life of Samuel Johnson, LL.D.*, by JAMES BOSWELL, Esq., the work to which this little book is a stepping-stone, Boswell claims that the story of Dr Johnson's life exhibits "a view of literature and literary men in Great-Britain, for near half a century, during which he flourished."

It is no idle claim. Indeed, Boswell might have gone a great deal further, for his story is not merely concerned with books and bookish men, but with men and women in every rank of society.

Kings and cottagers, statesmen and shopkeepers, bishops and play-actors, rich brewers and penniless poets, dukes and innkeepers, country parsons and gay young men of the town, street beggars and fashionable ladies—all play their part in the story and shew us a picture of the English world in the eighteenth century such as no history-book can give.

R. B. J.

Dr Johnson lived in four reigns—from 1709 to 1784. He could remember seeing Queen Anne and had an audience of George III; a Jacobite as a boy and a Tory always, he saw the '15 and the '45; he groaned under the Whig domination of Walpole and rejoiced in the Tory triumph of the king who gloried in the name of Briton; he saw the victories of our armies in India and Canada and their failure in America; he saw the damage done in the Gordon Riots and chatted to a South Sea islander brought home by Captain Cook; he dined with John Wilkes and was a guest in the house of Flora Macdonald.

In a tavern, a club, a drawing-room, or a post-chaise he would argue, and have the best of the argument, on the institution of slavery or the choice of books for babies; on the government of India or the poetry of Gray; on the doctrine of free will or the points of a bull-dog; on the manage-ment of a university press or the writing of a good cookery book.

In 1737 he came to London with twopence-halfpenny and a half-written tragedy in his pocket and for nearly twenty years did the work of an unknown literary drudge; for the last thirty years of his life he was the dominant figure in the edu-cated society of London, laying down the law on politics to Edmund Burke, on literature to Oliver Goldsmith, on painting to Sir Joshua Reynolds, on history to Edward Gibbon, on acting to David Garrick, and on everything to James Boswell.

Let us see what Boswell has to tell us.

School Days

JOHNSON was not born into the world at which we have just glanced. Indeed, had his character been less remarkable, he might have lived and died a schoolmaster, or a bookseller, in a country town. For his father, Michael Johnson, kept a bookshop in Lichfield, Staffordshire, and here his son Samuel was born in 1709.

Of old Mr Johnson Boswell says that "he was a pretty good Latin scholar, and a citizen so creditable as to be made one of the magistrates of Lichfield... He was a zealous high-church man and royalist and retained his attachment to the unfortunate house of Stuart."

Now, according to a modern poet:

> Every boy and every gal
> That's born into the world alive
> Is either a little Liberal
> Or else a little Conservative.

In those days men talked of Whig and Tory as we talk of Liberal and Conservative, and if ever a man was born a Tory, that man was Samuel Johnson.

To be a Tory in 1710 meant, generally speaking, to disapprove of the Revolution of 1688, when James II was driven from his throne and William III summoned to rule in his place; and great excitement had been caused in the country by a sermon preached at St Paul's against the principles of the Revolution by a certain Dr Sacheverell.

A visit of this preacher to Lichfield gave young Samuel Johnson the opportunity to shew himself what Boswell calls "the infant Hercules of Toryism." Here is the story told by a Lichfield lady:

"When Dr Sacheverel was at Lichfield, Johnson was not quite three years old. My grandfather Hammond observed him at the cathedral perched upon his father's shoulders, listening and gaping at the much celebrated preacher. Mr Hammond asked Mr Johnson how he could possibly think of bringing such an infant to church and in the midst of so great a croud. He answered, because it was impossible to keep him at home; for, young as he was, he believed he had caught the publick spirit and zeal for Sacheverel, and would have staid for ever in the church, satisfied with beholding him."

Nowadays it is difficult for us to imagine a three-year-old baby insisting on hearing a sermon, say, by the Dean of St Paul's or even a speech by the Prime Minister. But Johnson, as we shall see, was no ordinary child; and to the end of his life he was no ordinary hater of the Whigs.

Living, as he did, in the atmosphere of a book-shop, it was natural that the boy should be more inclined than others towards learning. His memory was wonderful:

"When he was a child in petticoats and had learnt to read, Mrs Johnson one morning put the common prayer-book into his hands, pointed

JOHNSON'S BIRTHPLACE AT LICHFIELD

to the collect for the day, and said 'Sam, you must get this by heart.' She went up stairs, leaving him to study it: But by the time she had reached the second floor, she heard him following her. 'What's the matter?' said she. 'I can say it,' he replied; and repeated it distinctly, though he could not have read it more than twice."

He was first taught to read English by one Dame Oliver and "from his earliest years he loved to read poetry, but hardly ever read any poem to the end;...he read Shakspeare at a period so early, that the speech of the Ghost in Hamlet terrified him when he was alone." At the age of 10 he began to learn Latin with an under master at Lichfield School, of which the headmaster, Mr Hunter, must have put terror into the hearts of his pupils.

"He used" so Johnson afterwards told Boswell "to beat us unmercifully; and he did not distinguish between ignorance and negligence; for he would beat a boy equally for not knowing a thing, as for neglecting to know it. He would ask a boy a question; and if he did not answer it, he would beat him, without considering whether he had an opportunity of knowing how to answer it. For instance, he would call up a boy and ask him Latin for a candlestick, which the boy could not expect to be asked. Now, Sir, if a boy could answer every question, there would be no need of a master to teach him."

"However..." says Boswell "Johnson was very sensible how much he owed to Mr Hunter. Mr Langton one day asked him how he had acquired

so accurate a knowledge of Latin, in which, I believe, he was exceeded by no man of his time; he
said 'My master whipt me very well. Without
that, Sir, I should have done nothing... A child
is afraid of being whipped and gets his task, and
there's an end on't.'"

Boswell also gives us a picture of Johnson at
school as drawn by a schoolfellow—Mr Hector:

"He seemed to learn by intuition...whenever
he made an exertion he did more than any one
else.... He was uncommonly inquisitive; and his
memory was so tenacious, that he never forgot anything that he either heard or read."

In the holidays Hector "could not oblige him
more than by sauntering away the hours of vacation
in the fields, during which he was more engaged
in talking to himself than to his companion."

This sounds more like a gloomy young prig
than a healthy 12-year-old boy. But Johnson was
far from healthy and his superior brains were useful to others besides himself:

"His favourites used to receive very liberal
assistance from him; and such was the submis-
sion and deference with which he was treated, such
the desire to obtain his regard, that three of the
boys, of whom Mr Hector was sometimes one,
used to come in the morning as his humble atten-
dants and carry him to school."

After a year at another school at Stourbridge,
he returned home:

"The two years which he spent at home, after
his return from Stourbridge, he passed in what he
thought idleness, and was scolded by his father for

his want of steady application. He had no settled plan of life, nor looked forward at all, but merely lived from day to day. Yet he read a great deal in a desultory manner, without any scheme of study, as chance threw books in his way, and inclination directed him through them. He used to mention one curious instance of his casual reading, when but a boy. Having imagined that his brother had hid some apples behind a large folio upon an upper shelf in his father's shop, he climbed up to search for them. There were no apples; but the large folio proved to be Petrarch, whom he had seen mentioned in some preface, as one of the restorers of learning. His curiosity having been thus excited, he sat down with avidity, and read a great part of the book. What he read during these two years he told me, was not works of mere amusement, 'not voyages and travels, but all literature, Sir, all ancient writers, all manly.'"

Johnson's father at this time used to set up a bookstall on market-days at neighbouring towns. One day he asked his son to go with him to Uttoxeter. Samuel refused, being too proud to stand at the stall in the market-place.

Again we feel inclined to think our hero rather a prig of a fellow—too lazy to do regular work of his own, too proud to help his father. Why couldn't he do a day's work and then spend his leisure in the open air, fishing or playing games?

Here we must go back a little and look at the sadder side of Johnson's boyhood. He was never healthy. From his father he inherited a "vile melancholy" and he "had the misfortune to be much afflicted with the scrophula, or king's evil, which disfigured a countenance naturally well formed, and hurt his visual nerves so much, that he did not see at all with one of his eyes, though its appearance was little different from that of the other."

At that time it was still believed that this disease could be cured by a touch of the reigning king or queen. So Mrs Johnson "carried him to London, where he was actually touched by Queen Anne...." Being asked if he could remember Queen Anne, "He had," he said, "a confused, but somehow a sort of solemn recollection of a lady in diamonds, and a long black hood."

But it did Johnson no good. Neither then, nor in later life, was he freed of the burden of ill-health and we can now better understand why "he never joined with the other boys in their ordinary diversions: his only amusement was in winter, when he took a pleasure in being drawn upon the ice by a boy barefooted, who pulled him along by a garter fixed round him; no very easy operation as his size was remarkably large. His defective sight, indeed, prevented him from enjoying the common sports."

Three habits, at least, Dr Johnson learned in boyhood which he continued to practise as a man —to hate the Whigs, to love books, and to endure pain.

Oxford and after

TWO hundred years ago it was not easy for a poor country bookseller to send his son to Oxford; and it is probable that it was only with the help of friends that old Mr Johnson was able to pay his son's expenses at the university.

However that may be, the name of Samuel Johnson was entered in the books of Pembroke College, Oxford, in 1728.

He had at least one parting gift, for good Dame Oliver, his first teacher, hearing that he was about to go, "came to take leave of him [and] brought him, in the simplicity of her kindness, a present of gingerbread, and said, he was the best scholar she ever had." Boswell further tells us that Johnson "delighted in mentioning this early compliment: adding, with a smile, that 'this was as high a proof of his merit as he could conceive.'"

Besides his gingerbread, however, Johnson took with him a good knowledge of books. ["I had looked" he said "into a great many books, which were not commonly known at the Universities, where they seldom read any books but what are put into their hands by their tutors; so that when I came to Oxford, Dr Adams told me I was the best qualified for the University that he had ever known come there."

And indeed he quickly showed himself to be more learned than the ordinary "freshman."

Nowadays, when a father takes his son for a first interview with a college tutor, it is not usual for the boy to break into the conversation with a quotation from one of the less-known Latin authors.

This is Boswell's story of Johnson's arrival at Oxford:

"His father, who had anxiously accompanied him, found means to have him introduced to Mr Jorden, who was to be his tutor....His father seemed very full of the merits of his son, and told the company he was a good scholar, and a poet, and wrote Latin verses. His figure and manner appeared strange to them; but he behaved modestly, and sat silent, till upon something which occurred in the course of conversation, he suddenly struck in and quoted Macrobius; and thus. he gave the first impression of that more extensive reading in which he had indulged himself." •

Johnson had no great opinion of Mr Jorden as a scholar:

"He was a very worthy man, but a heavy man, and I did not profit much by his instructions. Indeed, I did not attend him much. The first day after I came to college I waited upon him, and then stayed away four. On the sixth, Mr Jorden asked me why I had not attended. I answered I had been sliding in Christ Church meadow. And this I said with as much *nonchalance* as I am now talking to you. I had no notion I was wrong or irreverent to my tutor."

Johnson's rooms were on the second floor over the gateway of Pembroke College. The tower itself has been much altered, but the visitor to

Oxford can see the rooms pretty much as they were in Johnson's day. Elsewhere in the college he may examine (or "contemplate with veneration," as Boswell would have done) many Johnsonian relics—his writing-desk and tea-pot among them.

From what we already know of Johnson's boyhood, we cannot picture him as a lively undergraduate; for poverty and ill-health make it difficult for a young man to enjoy life with his fellows, and Johnson suffered from both.

A schoolfellow of Johnson, named Taylor, had come up to Christ Church, where one of the tutors, Mr Bateman, had a high reputation:

"Mr Bateman's lectures were so excellent, that Johnson used to come and get them at second-hand from Taylor, till his poverty being so extreme that his shoes were worn out, and his feet appeared through them, he saw that this humiliating circumstance was perceived by the Christ Church men, and he came no more. He was too proud to accept of money, and somebody having set a pair of new shoes at his door, he threw them away with indignation."

"How must we feel" adds the faithful Boswell "when we read such an anecdote of Samuel Johnson!"

Nor had his health improved. Here is an account of him at the end of his first year at Oxford:

"While he was at Lichfield, in the college vacation of the year 1729, he felt himself overwhelmed with...perpetual irritation, fretfulness and impatience; and with a dejection, gloom, and despair, which made existence misery. From this dismal malady he never afterwards was perfectly relieved...he was sometimes so languid and in-efficient, that he could not distinguish the hour upon the town-clock."

We are rather surprised, then, to read that he was at Oxford "caressed and loved by all about him, was a gay and frolicksome fellow, and passed there the happiest part of his life."

"This" says Boswell "is a striking proof of the fallacy of appearances, and how little any of us know of the real internal state even of those whom we see most frequently; for the truth is, that he was then depressed by poverty, and irri-tated by disease. When I mentioned to him this account as given me by Dr Adams, he said 'Ah, Sir, I was mad and violent. It was bitterness which they mistook for frolick. I was miserably poor, and I thought to fight my way by my literature and my wit; so I disregarded all power and all authority.'"

Johnson was too poor to complete his course of study and left Oxford in 1731 without the degree of Bachelor of Arts. But though he had no degree, he had gained much from the University. He had widened his knowledge of books, reading mostly Greek and Latin authors.

"He had" says Boswell "a peculiar facility in seizing at once what was valuable in any book, without submitting to the labour of perusing it from beginning to end."

He learnt, too, to love his college and the uni-versity. Later we shall see how affectionately he

talked of the days when "he was generally seen
lounging at the College gate, with a circle of
young students round him, whom he was entertaining with wit, and keeping from their studies."

"O! Mr Edwards!" he exclaimed to an old
friend about 50 years later "I'll convince you that
I recollect you. Do you remember our drinking
together at an alehouse near Pembroke gate?"
—but we must go back and see him as he came
down from Oxford at the age of 22:

"And now (I had almost said *poor*) Samuel
Johnson returned to his native city, destitute, and
not knowing how he should gain even a decent
livelihood. His father's misfortune in trade ren-
dered him unable to support his son; and for
some time there appeared no means by which he
could maintain himself. In the December of this
year his father died."

"I layed by" wrote Johnson in his diary (15 July
1732) "eleven guineas on this day, when I received twenty pounds, being all that I have reason
to hope for out of my father's effects, previous to
the death of my mother; an event which I pray
GOD may be very remote. I now therefore see
that I must make my own fortune."

How was this fortune to be made?

Like many another after him who has left the
university with no definite plan of life in view,
Johnson turned inevitably to teaching, accepting
"an offer to be employed as usher in the school of
Market-Bosworth, in Leicestershire, to which it
appears, from one of his little fragments of a diary,
that he went on foot."

Like many another, too, he soon complained that "this employment was very irksome to him in every respect...that it was unvaried as the note of the cuckow; and that he did not know whether it was more disagreeable for him to teach, or the boys to learn, the grammar rules."

A few months of this were enough for him, after which he went to live with his friend Mr Hector at Birmingham and began to earn a little money by his pen. For the translation of a French book of travel he received five guineas.

In Birmingham Johnson fell in love with a widow—Mrs Porter. This lady was twice her lover's age and, as we shall see in a moment, no great beauty.

Nor was Johnson. When he was first introduced to her, "his appearance was very forbidding; he was then lean and lank, so that his immense structure of bones was hideously striking to the eye, and the scars of the scrophula were deeply visible. He also wore his hair, which was straight and stiff, and separated behind: and he often had, seemingly, convulsive starts and odd gesticulations, which tended to excite at once surprize and ridicule. Mrs Porter was so much engaged by his conversation that she overlooked all these external disadvantages and said to her daughter, 'this is the most sensible man that I ever saw in my life.'"

"I know not" Boswell goes on "for what reason the marriage ceremony was not performed at Birmingham; but a resolution was taken that it should be at Derby, for which place the bride and bridegroom set out on horseback, I suppose in very good humour...I have had from my illustrious friend the following curious account of their journey to church upon the nuptial morn: 'Sir, she had read the old romances, and had got into her head the fantastical notion that a woman of spirit should use her lover like a dog. So, Sir, at first she told me that I rode too fast, and she could not keep up with me; and, when I rode a little slower, she passed me, and complained that I lagged behind. I was not to be made the slave of caprice; and I resolved to begin as I meant to end. I therefore pushed on briskly, till I was fairly out of her sight. The road lay between two hedges, so I was sure she could not miss it; and I contrived that she should soon come up with me. When she did, I observed her to be in tears.'"

This is what Boswell, who was a married man, calls "a manly firmness," though he admits that it was "a singular beginning."

"Sir," said Johnson to a friend years afterwards "it was a love marriage on both sides."

"In the *Gentleman's Magazine* for 1736," says Boswell, "there is the following advertisement:

'At Edial, near Lichfield, in Staffordshire, young gentlemen are boarded and taught the Latin and Greek languages, by SAMUEL JOHNSON.'

But the only pupils that were put under his care were the celebrated David Garrick and his brother George, and a Mr Offely, a young gentleman of good fortune who died early."

Boswell (though he has a kind word of patronage for successful schoolmasters) evidently thought

that his hero's brains were too good, and his temper too bad, for the profession of teaching; moreover, David Garrick was the kind of boy who is
the despair of his teacher, the delight of his school-
fellows, and the hero of school stories.

The truth about Johnson as a schoolmaster,
according to Boswell, was that "he was not so well
qualified for being a teacher of elements...as men
of inferiour powers of mind...The art of commu-
nicating instruction, of whatever kind, is much to
be valued; and I have ever thought that those
who devote themselves to this employment, and
do their duty with diligence and success, are en-
titled to very high respect from the community,
as Johnson himself often maintained. Yet I am
of opinion that the greatest abilities are not only
not required for this office, but render a man less
fit for it. While we acknowledge the justness of
Thomson's beautiful remark,

'Delightful task! to rear the tender thought,
And teach the young idea how to shoot!'

we must consider that this delight is perceptible
only by 'a mind at ease,' a mind at once calm
and clear; but that a mind gloomy and impetuous
like that of Johnson, cannot be fixed for any length
of time in minute attention, and must be so
frequently irritated by unavoidable slowness and
errour in the advances of scholars, as to perform
the duty, with little pleasure to the teacher, and
no great advantage to the pupils. Good temper
is a most essential requisite in a Preceptor....
From Mr Garrick's account he did not appear
to have been profoundly reverenced by his pupils.

His oddities of manner, and uncouth gesticulations, could not but be the subject of merriment... and, in particular, the young rogues used to... turn into ridicule his tumultuous and awkward fondness for Mrs Johnson, whom he used to name ...*Tetty* or *Tetsey*...which seems to us ludicrous, when applied to a woman of her age and appearance. Mr Garrick described her to me as very fat, with a bosom of more than ordinary protuberance, with swelled cheeks of a florid red, produced by thick painting, and increased by the liberal use of cordials; flaring and fantastick in her dress, and affected both in her speech and her general behaviour. I have seen Garrick exhibit her, by his exquisite talent of mimickry, so as to excite the heartiest bursts of laughter."

The "exquisite talent of mimickry" is not popular amongst schoolmasters and the academy for young gentlemen was closed after a year and a half.

Again, what was Johnson to do? He had tried teaching and failed; he had written a little, but could not hope to get money or fame by selling translations to country booksellers; he had married a wife. The next step was the decisive one:

"Johnson now thought of trying his fortune in London."

R. B. J.

Johnson comes to London

"I CAME to London" said Johnson in later years "with two-pence half-penny in my pocket."

Garrick overhearing him, exclaimed, "eh? what do you say? with two-pence half-penny in your pocket?"

JOHNSON, "Why yes; when I came with two-pence half-penny in *my* pocket, and thou, Davy, with three half-pence in thine."

Master and pupil had travelled together; Garrick was to 'complete his education' at an academy kept by a Mr Colson, but it was well for Johnson that he "knew how he could live in the cheapest manner. His first lodgings were at the house of Mr Norris, a staymaker, in Exeter-street, adjoining Catherine-street, in the Strand. 'I dined (said he) very well for eight-pence, with very good company, at the Pine Apple in New-street, just by. Several of them had travelled. They expected to meet every day; but did not know one another's names. It used to cost the rest a shilling, for they drank wine; but I had a cut of meat for six-pence, and bread for a penny, and gave the waiter a penny; so that I was quite well served, nay, better than the rest, for they gave the waiter nothing.'"

Johnson was, as Boswell says, "an adventurer in

literature." What kind of place was this London of 1737, this "great field of genius and exertion, where" according to Boswell "talents of every kind have the fullest scope, and the highest encouragement"?

Here are two pictures. The first is an account of an ordinary day's doings by a stranger staying in Pall Mall:

"We rise by nine, and those that frequent great men's levees find entertainment at them till eleven or go to tea-tables. About twelve the *beau monde* assembles in several coffee or chocolate houses... all so near to one another that in less than an hour you see the company of them all. We are carried to these places in chairs, which are here very cheap, a guinea a week, or one shilling per hour, and your chair-men serve you for porters to run on errands... If it is fine weather we take a turn in the park till two, when we go for dinner... Ordinaries are not so common here as abroad, but there are good French ones in Suffolk Street. The general way here is to make a party at the coffee-house to go to dine at the tavern, where we sit till six, when we go to the play, except you are invited to the table of some great man. After the play the best company generally go to Tom's and Will's coffee-houses near adjoining, where there is playing at picquet and the best of conversation till midnight.... Or if you like rather the company of ladies, there are assemblies at most people of quality's houses."

The second is by an Irish painter whom Johnson had met at Birmingham and who had "practised his own precepts of œconomy for several years in the British capital":

"He assured Johnson, who, I suppose, was then meditating to try his fortune in London, but was apprehensive of the expence, that thirty pounds a year was enough to enable a man to live there without being contemptible. He allowed ten pounds for clothes and linen. He said a man might live in a garret at eighteen-pence a week; few people would enquire where he lodged; and, if they did, it was easy to say 'Sir, I am to be found at such a place.' By spending three-pence in a coffee-house, he might be for some hours every day in very good company; he might dine for sixpence, breakfast on bread and milk for a penny, and do without supper. On *clean-shirt-day* he went abroad, and paid visits."

It was this world of "Grub Street" (a street which became famous about the end of the 16th century as the home of poor authors and whose name was used generally to mean the world in which they lived[1]) which Johnson had to face. He must try and make a living by his pen.

He had, of course, no "patron," no rich man who would help to pay for the printing of his books, recommend them to his fashionable friends and perhaps secure their author a government post which would bring with it light duties and a comfortable income.

Except for Harry Hervey ("a vicious man, but very kind to me," he told Boswell, "If you call a dog HERVEY, I shall love him") Johnson hardly

1 See pages 33, 95.

had a friend in London. What was he to write? Who was to buy his manuscripts?

Newspapers, indeed, were everywhere. They consisted mostly of four pages containing a little news, a little gossip, a little poetry, and many advertisements. There was not much hope for Johnson here.

A journal founded in 1731 gave him a better opening.

" *The Gentleman's Magazine*, begun and carried on by Mr Edward Cave, under the name of SYLVANUS URBAN, had attracted the notice and esteem of Johnson, in an eminent degree, before he came to London.... He told me, that when he first saw St John's Gate, the place where that deservedly popular miscellany was originally printed, he 'beheld it with reverence.'"

To Mr Cave, therefore, Johnson wrote, having observed in his paper "very uncommon offers of encouragement to men of letters," and *The Gentleman's Magazine* was for many years "his principal source for employment and support."

In the summer of 1737 he went back to Lichfield, where he finished a tragedy called *Irene*, of which we shall hear something later. On his return to London he brought his wife with him, and in London he lived for the remaining 47 years of his life.

It was fitting, therefore, that the first of his writings which brought him fame should be a poem called *London*. It was offered to, and refused by, several booksellers, an incident afterwards commemorated in these lines:

Will no kind patron JOHNSON own?
Shall JOHNSON friendless range the town?
And every publisher refuse
The offspring of his happy Muse?

However, the "worthy, modest, and ingenious Mr Robert Dodsley had taste enough to perceive its uncommon merit, and thought it creditable to have a share in it."

Now this poem may not attract us very much to-day. Boswell, of course, thought it "one of the noblest productions in our language," but to understand it properly we need to know something of the politics of the time, especially of the Tory feeling against Sir Robert Walpole, the prime minister who said that "every man had his price"; we need to know something, too, of the poem by Juvenal, of which it is an imitation.

But a few lines are quoted here, because they bring out very clearly the state of Johnson's mind at the time.

He is a bitter opponent of the corrupt government of the day and its weak concessions to Spain:

Grant me, kind heaven, to find some happier place,
Where honesty and sense are no disgrace...
Here let those reign, whom pensions can incite
To vote a patriot black, a courtier white;
Explain their country's dear-bought rights away,
And plead for pirates in the face of day[1].

---

[1] The Spaniards had abused the right of searching merchant vessels granted to them by the treaty of Commerce. . In the following year, 1739, after the affair of "Jenkins's ear," Walpole was compelled to yield to the popular demand for war.

The *Gentleman's* Magazine:

St JOHN's GATE.

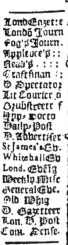

Lond Gazette
Londō Journ
Fog's Journ.
Applebee's ::
Read's : : : :
Craftsman : :
© Spectator
Lit Courier o
Grubstreet f
App. Porto
Daily Post
D. Advertiser
St James's Ch.
Whitehall Ev
Lond. Even'g
Weekly Mise
General Eve.
Old Whig
D. Gazetteer
Lon. E. Post
Com. Sense.

York News
Dublin f : :
Edinburgh 2
Bristol : : : :
Norwich 2
Exeter 2 : : :
Worcester
Northampton
Gloucester : :
Stamford : :
Nottingham
Bury Journ.
Chester ditto
Derby ditto
Ipswich ba.
Reading bo.
Leeds Merc.
Newcastle
Canterbury
Durham
Kendal
Boston : ¶
Barbados :
Jamaica &c

For MARCH, 1738.

CONTAINING,

More in Quantity, and greater Variety than any Book of the Kind and Price.

I. Original Pieces in great Variety: As 1. The Lady's Adventures, Part I. concluded. 2. The first Sin of the fallen Angels, their Breach of a Covenant. By R. Y. 3. Tythes opposed, and defended. 4. Difficult Places in Scripture explained, and others proposed. 5. Milton's PARADISE LOST censured. 6. The Christian Revelation set in a new Light, so as to be one of the strongest Proofs of natural Religion. 7. Of the Quantity of the Refraction of Light in the Moon's Atmosphere. By Mr FACIO. With Cutts, &c.

II. Some of the most curious Weekly ESSAYS, viz. Of contemplative Enthusiasm, or Superstition, with a Parallel between the two Branches of Enthusiasm. Vindication of a young M——r of P——t. The Temple of

DETRACTION. Tragical Effects of AVARICE. Of the *Spanish Guarda Costas*. Conclusion of the Bishop of *Gloucester's* Sermon before the Lords, &c.

III. POETRY: The Volunteer Laureat, No. 7. By *Richard Savage*, Esq; Poem by a *Welch* Curate on his native Country. *In obitum* Georgii *Ducis* Albemarlii, *Authore* R. Allestree, S. T. F. The Pleasures of *Jamaica*. To the E. of *Orrery*; by the Rev. Mr *Trevanian*. 107 Psalm Paraphras'd, by LYDIA. On M. URBAN's Adversaries. By SYLVIUS and others, &c.

IV. HISTORICAL CHRONICLE.
V. List of Ships taken by the *Spaniards*.
VI. FOREIGN Transactions.
VII. REGISTER of Books.
VIII. TABLE of CONTENTS.

By *SYLVANUS URBAN*, Gent.

LONDON · Printed by E. CAVE at St JOHN's GATE, and Sold by the Bookfellers of Town and Country; of whom may be had any former Month. also complete Sets on Royal or Common Paper beginning with the Year 1731 and a Supplement for the Year 1737, with a Map of the Garden of *Eden*.

TITLE-PAGE OF *The Gentleman's Magazine*, March, 1738

He feels his own poverty keenly:

This mournful truth is ev'rywhere confess'd
SLOW RISES WORTH, BY POVERTY DEPRESS'D.

"We may easily conceive" says Boswell "with what feeling a great mind like this, cramped and galled by narrow circumstances, uttered this last line, which he marked by capitals."

London was a success.

"Everybody was delighted with it; and there being no name to it, the first buz of the literary circles was 'here is an unknown poet, greater even than Pope.' And it is recorded in *The Gentleman's Magazine* of that year [1738], that it 'got into the second edition in the course of a week.'"

But Johnson got no more than ten guineas for his work.

Truly, as Boswell says, "he felt the hardships of writing for bread." So poor, indeed, did his prospects seem, that he thought of turning schoolmaster again or of entering the law. But he had no university degree and there seemed no escape from "the drudgery of authourship"—unless he should take the advice of Mr Wilcox.

"Mr Wilcox, the bookseller, on being informed by him that his intention was to get his livelihood as an author, eyed his robust frame attentively, and with a significant look, said 'You had better buy a porter's knot.'"

Of his life during the first ten years after his arrival in London we do not know many details. He was miserably poor, but not entirely friendless. His intimate companion for some time was Richard Savage, whom "misfortunes and miscon-

duct had reduced to the lowest state of wretched-
ness as a writer for bread."

Boswell finds it "melancholy to reflect that
Johnson and Savage were sometimes in such extreme indigence that they could not pay for a
lodging; so that they have wandered together
whole nights in the streets.... He told Sir Joshua
Reynolds, that one night in particular, when
Savage and he walked round St James's-square
for want of a lodging, they were not at all depressed
by their situation; but in high spirits and brimful
of patriotism, traversed the square for several
hours, inveighed against the minister, and 'resolved they would *stand by their country*.'"

A few years later Johnson wrote a *Life* of his
friend, sitting up all night and writing forty-eight
of the printed pages at a sitting.

"Soon after Savage's *Life* was published, Mr
Harte dined with Edward Cave, and occasionally
praised it. Soon after, meeting him, Cave said,
'You made a man very happy t'other day.'–'How
could that be?' says Harte; 'nobody was there
but ourselves.' Cave answered, by reminding him
that a plate of victuals was sent behind a screen,
which was to Johnson, dressed so shabbily, that
he did not choose to appear; but on hearing the
conversation, he was highly delighted with the
encomiums on his book."

For the copyright of the book Johnson received
fifteen guineas.

Such money, indeed, as Johnson earned at this
time came mostly from Mr Cave. To *The Gentleman's Magazine* he contributed poems, essays,

lives of famous men, translations of foreign works and accounts of debates in Parliament, taking care, in these last, that "the WHIG DOGS should not have the best of it."

Few of these writings would be remembered if their author had not become famous for other reasons, and we may be sure that Johnson was dissatisfied with this kind of work. He was an adventurer in literature and an adventurer likes to tackle a big task.

Before long he found one big enough.

The Great Lexicographer

THE title of this chapter sounds dull enough. A dictionary is not generally thought to be lively reading and perhaps we may feel that a man who deliberately set out to write one must have been a dry-as-dust old fellow who went out of his way to explain short and simple words by means of long and complicated phrases more difficult than the words themselves.

Well, there is no doubt that Johnson did use long words. He had been brought up on classical authors and, like other writers of the period, often used words of many syllables derived from the Greek or Latin, when simpler words would have done as well.

Boswell is the same. He does not say "many times in his later life" but "upon innumerable occasions in his subsequent life." Or look back at page 24, where he finds it "melancholy to reflect that Johnson and Savage were in such extreme indigence." Why couldn't he have found it "sad to think that they were so poor"?

Long words were the fashion of the time and to do Johnson justice, we must try to put ourselves back in his century.

Nowadays, we have no trouble in finding dictionaries, whether we want an exhaustive work of reference or a handy volume for the pocket.

But in Johnson's day it was different.

Such dictionaries as had previously appeared were vocabularies of "hard words" only, not of words in general. The only attempt to produce a dictionary containing *all* English words was that compiled in 1721 by one Nathaniel Bailey, but it contained very little illustration of the use of words. There was, in fact, no dictionary which attempted either to *fix* the language or to illustrate the different meanings of a word by quotations from English writers. Johnson began to consider whether he might not produce one himself.

"The year 1747" says Boswell "is distinguished as the epoch, when Johnson's arduous and important work, his DICTIONARY OF THE ENGLISH LANGUAGE, was announced to the world, by the publication of its Plan or *Prospectus*. How long this immense undertaking had been the object of his contemplation, I do not know. I once asked him by what means he had attained to that astonishing knowledge of our language, by which he was enabled to realise a design of such extent, and accumulated difficulty. He told me, that 'it was not the effect of particular study; but that it had grown up in his mind insensibly.'"

Even Johnson had had some doubts at the beginning:

"I have been informed by Mr James Dodsley, that several years before this period, when Johnson was one day sitting in his brother Robert's shop, he heard his brother suggest to him, that a Dictionary of the English Language would be a work that would be well received by the publick; that Johnson seemed at first to catch at the proposition, but, after a pause, said, in his abrupt decisive manner, 'I believe I shall not undertake it.'"

But he changed his mind. Half-a-dozen book-sellers agreed between them to pay the author fifteen hundred and seventy-five pounds for the work, and the "Plan" was addressed to the Earl of Chesterfield, "then one of his Majesty's Principal Secretaries of State; a nobleman who was very ambitious of literary distinction."

England has always prided herself on the individual enterprise of her citizens and Johnson "the true-born Englishman" had now undertaken, "single and unaided...a work which in other countries had not been effected but by the co-operating exertions of many," but "he had a noble consciousness of his own abilities, which enabled him to go on with undaunted spirit."

Boswell gives us a few glimpses of his hero engaged on this great task:

"Dr Adams found him one day busy at his *Dictionary*, when the following dialogue ensued: ADAMS. This is a great work, Sir…How can you do this in three years? JOHNSON. Sir, I have no doubt that I can do it in three years. ADAMS. But the French Academy, which consists of forty members, took forty years to compile their Dictionary. JOHNSON. Sir, thus it is: this is the proportion. Let me see; forty times forty is sixteen hundred. As three to sixteen hundred, so is the proportion of an Englishman to a Frenchman."

"For the mechanical part he employed, as he told me, six amanuenses; and let it be remembered by the natives of North-Britain, to whom he is supposed to have been so hostile, that five of them were of that country…. To all these painful labourers, Johnson shewed a never-ceasing kindness."

"While the *Dictionary* was going forward, Johnson lived part of the time in Holborn, part in Gough-square, Fleet-street; and he had an upper room fitted up like a counting-house for the purpose, in which he gave to the copyists their several tasks. The words, partly taken from other dictionaries, and partly supplied by himself, having been first written down with spaces left between them, he delivered in writing their etymologies, definitions, and various significations. The authorities were copied from the books themselves, in which he had marked the passages, with a black-lead pencil, the traces of which could easily be effaced. I have seen several of them, in which that trouble had not been taken, so that they were just as when used by the copyists."

Johnson's house in Gough Square

Though these pencil-marks do not remain for us to see, the house in Gough Square still stands. The literary adventurer of to-day may behold it with something of that reverence which St John's Gate inspired in Johnson when he first came to London.

The Dictionary employed Johnson for eight years.

"Mr Andrew Millar, bookseller in the Strand, took the principal charge of conducting the publication.... When the messenger who carried the last sheet to Millar returned, Johnson asked him 'Well, what did he say?'—'Sir (answered the messenger) he said, Thank GOD I have done with him.' 'I am glad (replied Johnson, with a smile) that he thanks GOD for anything.'"

Lord Chesterfield, to whom the "Plan" had been addressed, had taken no notice of Johnson during his years of toil. Johnson had waited in his "outward rooms" and been "repulsed from his door"—an incident which a famous picture has made familiar to many who otherwise, perhaps, would hardly have heard either of the rich nobleman or of the "uncourtly scholar."

On the eve of publication, however, Lord Chesterfield attempted to make amends by two complimentary notices in a paper called *The World*. This provoked Johnson to write one of the best known letters in English literature. Here is a part of it:

"Seven years, my Lord, have now passed, since I waited in your outward rooms, or was repulsed from your door; during which time I have been pushing on my work through difficulties, of which it is useless to complain, and have brought it, at last, to the verge of publication, without one act of assistance, one word of encouragement, or one smile of favour. Such treatment I did not expect, for I never had a Patron before....

Is not a Patron, my Lord, one who looks with unconcern on a man struggling for life in the water, and, when he has reached ground, encumbers him with help? The notice which you have been pleased to take of my labours, had it been early, had been kind; but it has been delayed till I am indifferent, and cannot enjoy it; till I am solitary, and cannot impart it; till I am known, and do not want it. I hope it is no very cynical asperity not to confess obligations where no benefit has been received, or to be unwilling that the Publick should consider me as owing that to a Patron, which Providence has enabled me to do for myself."

This fine piece of snubbing, written, as Johnson said, in *defensive* pride, became "the talk of the town." But Johnson did not wish it to be public property. When Lord Hardwicke expressed a wish to read it, he "declined to comply with the request, saying, with a smile 'No, Sir; I have hurt the dog too much already.'"

"The *Dictionary*" says Boswell "with a *Grammar and History of the English Language* being now at length published, in two volumes folio, the world contemplated with wonder so stupendous a work achieved by one man."

We, too, may do the same, though we may be frightened, rather than attracted, by the sentence which Boswell selects from the *Preface* as a model of clearness and choice of words:

"When the radical idea branches out into parallel ramifications, how can a consecutive series be formed of senses in their own nature collateral?"

We shall do better to choose one or two of the passages which should move us even now, when we picture to ourselves the years of industry and poverty in the gloomy Gough Square house: "The chief glory of every people arises from its authors: whether I shall add anything by my own writings to the reputation of English literature must be left to time."

"I deliver my book to the world with the spirit of a man that has endeavoured well.... In this work, when it shall be found that much is omitted, let it not be forgotten that much likewise is performed; and though no book was ever spared out of tenderness to the author, and the world is little solicitous to know whence proceeded the faults of that which it condemns; yet it may gratify curiosity to inform it, that the *English Dictionary* was written with little assistance of the learned, and without any patronage of the great; not in the soft obscurities of retirement, or under the shelter of academick bowers, but amidst inconvenience and distraction, in sickness and in sorrow."

The Dictionary itself is not, of course, to be compared in fulness or accuracy with the latest monument of lexicography which we find on library shelves to-day—any more than Marlborough's artillery can be compared with a modern howitzer.

"The definitions" says Boswell "have always appeared to me such astonishing proofs of acuteness of intellect and precision of language, as indicate a genius of the highest rank. This it is which marks the superiour excellence of Johnson's *Dictionary* over others."

But even Boswell has to admit, as Johnson did, that there are errors and obscurities, "inconsiderable specks" though they be.

"Thus *Windward* and *Leeward*, though directly of opposite meaning, are defined identically the same way."

"A lady once asked him how he came to define *Pastern* the *knee* of a horse; instead of making an elaborate defence, as she expected, he at once answered, 'Ignorance, Madam,—pure ignorance.'"

"His definition of *Network* has been often quoted with sportive malignity, as obscuring a thing in itself very plain."

Boswell tantalises us by omitting this definition. But, to set curiosity at rest, here it is: "Anything reticulated or decussated, at equal distances, with interstices between the intersections."

A man of strong prejudices like Johnson could not refrain from letting his own views appear here and there throughout the work and it is these human touches which have most attraction for us to-day. We can imagine the grim smile which came over his scarred and rugged face when he defined:

Oats as "A grain which in England is generally

given to horses, but in Scotland supports the people[1]."

Whig as "The name of a faction."

Grub-street as "the name of a street in London, much inhabited by writers of small histories, *dictionaries*, and temporary poems."

Lexicographer as "a writer of dictionaries; a harmless drudge."

"Dictionaries," as Johnson himself wrote thirty years later, "are like watches, the worst is better than none, and the best cannot be expected to go true."

But what we chiefly have to remember is that Johnson was a pioneer. There was no good English dictionary in 1747. Johnson set to work single-handed, and produced a book which made its author supreme amongst the literary men of the time and itself remained a standard work for generations.

The Great Cham of Literature

THE *Dictionary* was Johnson's biggest literary adventure, but it was not the only one which occupied him in the years between 1747 and 1755. Even the great Lexicographer would have found it hard to do nothing but "beat the track

---

[1] The latter part of the definition was omitted by Johnson in the last edition which he passed for press.

of the alphabet" for eight years; for, as Boswell puts it, "his enlarged and lively mind could not be satisfied without more diversity of employment and the pleasure of animated relaxation."

There was another reason, too, which made it necessary for Johnson to write something besides definitions. 1500 guineas was not much on which to keep six assistants and himself for eight years. "When the expence of amanuenses and paper, and other articles are deducted, his clear profit was very inconsiderable." But Johnson, being a true adventurer, did not grumble. When Boswell said to him "I am sorry, Sir, you did not get more for your *Dictionary*," his answer was "I am sorry too. But it was very well. The booksellers are generous, liberal-minded men."

So, in 1749, Johnson offered to one of these booksellers, Mr James Dodsley, a poem called *The Vanity of Human Wishes* and received the sum of fifteen guineas.

It was written in imitation, as *London* had been, of the Roman poet Juvenal. The subject is a gloomy one and Garrick thought it "as hard as Greek." But parts of the poem are still familiar to everyone—the opening lines, for instance:

> Let observation with extensive view
> Survey mankind, from China to Peru.

Various ambitious careers are described, such as those of Wolsey and Charles XII of Sweden; and a bitter warning is given to the literary adventurer, "the young enthusiast" who "quits his ease for fame."

Deign on the passing world to turn thine eyes,
And pause awhile from letters, to be wise;
There mark what ills the scholar's life assail,
Toil, envy, want, the patron[1], and the jail.

David Garrick was by this time a famous actor. He was manager of Drury Lane theatre, and, after a good deal of dispute, it was arranged that Johnson's tragedy *Irene*, written some years before, should be put upon the stage. It was a play dealing with an Oriental court and Garrick was rehearsing the part of Mahomet.

"'Sir' said Johnson to a friend, 'the fellow wants me to make Mahomet run mad, that he may have an opportunity of tossing his hands and kicking his heels.'"

Here is an account of the first night:

"Before the curtain drew up, there were cat-calls whistling, which alarmed Johnson's friends. The Prologue, which was written by himself in a manly strain, soothed the audience, and the play went off tolerably, till it came to the conclusion, when Mrs Pritchard, the heroine of the piece, was to be strangled upon the stage, and was to speak two lines with the bow-string round her neck. The audience cried out '*Murder! Murder!*' She several times attempted to speak; but in vain. At last she was obliged to go off the stage alive."

This was Johnson's one adventure as a writer of plays and he no doubt enjoyed it. Everyone loves to go "behind the scenes."

"His necessary attendance while his play was

---

[1] Johnson originally wrote *garret*, but, after his treatment by Lord Chesterfield, altered it to *patron*.

in rehearsal, and during its performance, brought him acquainted with many of the performers of both sexes....With some of them he kept up an acquaintance as long as he and they lived, and was ever ready to shew them acts of kindness. He for a considerable time used to frequent the *Green Room*, and seemed to take delight in dissipating his gloom, by mixing in the sprightly chit-chat of the motley circle then to be found there."

He felt, too, that his own dress should be in keeping with the gay clothes of those around him:

"On occasion of his play being brought upon the stage, Johnson had a fancy that as a dramatick authour his dress should be more gay than what he ordinarily wore; he therefore appeared behind the scenes, and even in one of the side boxes, in a scarlet waistcoat, with rich gold lace, and a gold-laced hat."

But *Irene* was not a success.

"Notwithstanding all the support of such performers as Garrick, Barry, Mrs Cibber, Mrs Pritchard, and every advantage of dress and decoration, the tragedy of *Irene* did not please the publick." However "Mr Garrick's zeal carried it through for nine nights, so that the authour had his three nights' profits."

These, together with the hundred pounds which Johnson received from Mr Dodsley for the copyright, made it, at any rate, a profitable adventure and "when asked how he felt upon the ill success of his tragedy, he replied, 'Like the Monument'; meaning that he continued firm and unmoved as that column."

In the following year, 1750, he set out upon another adventure. It was nearly forty years since the last numbers of *The Tatler* and *The Spectator*, written by the famous essayists of Queen Anne's reign—Joseph Addison and Richard Steele— had appeared.

Johnson now embarked upon a similar periodical paper in which, as Boswell says, "he came forth as a majestick teacher of moral and religious wisdom."

The choice of a title gave him some trouble: "What *must* be done, Sir," he afterwards told Sir Joshua Reynolds "*will* be done. When I was to begin publishing that paper, I was at a loss how to name it. I sat down at night upon my bedside, and resolved that I would not go to sleep till I had fixed its title. *The Rambler* seemed the best that occurred, and I took it."

"The first paper of the *Rambler*" Boswell tells us "was published on Tuesday the 20th of March 1750; and its authour was enabled to continue it, without interruption, every Tuesday and Friday, till Saturday[1] the 17th of March, 1752, on which day it closed....Many of these discourses, which we should suppose had been laboured with all the slow attention of literary leisure, were written in haste as the moment pressed, without even being read over by him before they were printed."

Like *Irene*, *The Rambler* did not really "please the publick." The matter was too solid for a two-penny paper, and less than 500 copies of each

[1] This Saturday was in fact 14 March.

number were sold. Boswell speaks sadly of this lack of success:

"The grave and often solemn cast of thinking, which distinguished it from other periodical papers, made it, for some time, not generally liked. So slowly did this excellent work, of which twelve editions have now issued from the press, gain upon the world at large, that even in the closing number the authour says, 'I have never been much a favourite with the publick.'"

But from one source, at any rate, Johnson got honest praise:

"Mrs Johnson, in whose judgement and taste he had great confidence, said to him, after a few numbers of the *Rambler* had come out 'I thought very well of you before; but I did not imagine you could have written anything equal to this.'"

"Distant praise, from whatever quarter," adds Boswell "is not so delightful as that of a wife whom a man loves and esteems."

Johnson was now emerging from the period of "cold obscurity." He had begun to gather a circle of friends round him and had founded the first of his clubs "in Ivy-lane, Paternoster-row, with a view to enjoy literary discussion, and amuse his evening hours." His character, though not his income, in the literary world was "deservedly high" and one honour which came to him in 1754 was especially pleasing to him—the conferment of the degree of Master of Arts by the University of Oxford. We can see how much he looked forward to this by a phrase in one of his letters at the time: "I shall be extremely glad to hear from you again, to know if the affair [of the degree] proceeds. I have mentioned it to none of my friends for fear of being laughed at for my disappointment."

"In 1755 we behold him" says Boswell "to great advantage; his degree of Master of Arts conferred upon him, his *Dictionary* published, his correspondence animated, his benevolence exercised." But in the following year "Johnson found that the great fame of his *Dictionary* had not set him above the necessity of 'making provision for the day that was passing over him.' No royal or noble patron extended a munificent hand to give independence to the man who had conferred stability on the language of his country."

In other words, he must still write for a living. "Ten guineas" he afterwards said "was to me at that time a great sum" and he did not disdain to accept a guinea from Mr Robert Dodsley, "for writing the introduction to *The London Chronicle*, an evening news-paper."

He tried his hand, too, at another series of essays which, under the name of *The Idler*, came out every Saturday in a weekly newspaper. Boswell says that these essays have "less body and more spirit" than *The Rambler* and refers to one "in which conversation is assimilated to a bowl of punch." Many of them were written "as hastily as an ordinary letter."

"Mr Langton remembers Johnson, when on a visit at Oxford, asking him one evening how long it was till the post went out; and on being told about half an hour, he exclaimed, 'then we 'shall do very well.' He upon this instantly sat down and finished an *Idler*, which it was necessary should be in London the next day. Mr Langton having signified a wish to read it, 'Sir, (said he) you shall not do more than I have done myself.' He then folded it up and sent it off."

Johnson, at the age of 49, was still writing in the spirit of the journalist.

A more ambitious work was *Rasselas, Prince of Abyssinia*, a tale of the East. This became very popular and was "translated into most, if not all, of the modern languages." It was written in the same hurried and casual way as *The Rambler* and *The Idler*:

"Johnson wrote it, that with the profits he might defray the expence of his mother's funeral, and pay some little debts which she had left.' He told Sir Joshua Reynolds that he had composed it in the evenings of one week, sent it to the press in portions as it was written, and had never since read it over. Mr Strahan, Mr Johnston, and Mr Dodsley purchased it for a hundred pounds, but afterwards paid him twenty-five pounds more, when it came to a second edition."

Besides these works and an edition of Shakespeare which employed him for many years, Johnson wrote a number of essays, reviews of books, prefaces and dedications. From one of these, a defence of tea-drinking, we must quote a sentence later, for Boswell gives it as his opinion that "his chief Intention seems to have been to make Sport."

And now Johnson's career as "an adventurer

in literature" is nearly at an end. What is, in some ways, the most important event of his life is thus described by Boswell:

"The accession of George the Third to the throne of these kingdoms, opened a new and brighter prospect to men of literary merit, who had been honoured with no mark of royal favour in the preceding reign. His present Majesty's education in this country, as well as his taste and beneficence, prompted him to be patron of science and the arts; and early this year Johnson, having been represented to him as a very learned and good man, without any certain provision, his Majesty was pleased to grant him a pension of three hundred pounds a year."

Johnson, being an honest man, had some qualms. In the two previous reigns he had been bitterly opposed to the government and had not hesitated to say so. Moreover, he had defined *Pension* in his Dictionary as "pay given to a state hireling for treason to his country[1]"! Could he honestly take the money? He went off at once to consult Sir Joshua Reynolds:

"Sir Joshua answered that...there could be no objection to his receiving from the King a reward for literary merit; and that certainly the definitions in his *Dictionary* were not applicable to him. Johnson, it should seem, was satisfied, for he did not call again till he had accepted the pension, and had waited on Lord Bute[2] to thank him. He

---

[1] This was omitted in later editions and the following version retained: "A slave of state hired by a stipend to obey his master." See also the lines quoted from *London*, page 22.

[2] The Prime Minister.

then told Sir Joshua that Lord Bute said to him expressly, 'It is not given you for anything to do, but for what you have done.' His Lordship, he said, behaved in the handsomest manner. He repeated the words twice, that he might be sure Johnson heard them, and thus set his mind perfectly at ease."

No one was ever more fervently grateful than Johnson, who at the age of 53, had never known a day's good health or a year's steady income. He, who had compiled the Dictionary, declared:

"The English language does not afford me terms adequate to my feelings on this occasion. I must have recourse to the French. I am *pénétré* with his Majesty's goodness."

Twenty years later his gratitude was still fresh:

"Sir, I have never complained of the world; nor do I think that I have reason to complain. It is rather to be wondered at that I have so much. My pension is more out of the usual course of things than any instance that I have known. Here, Sir, was a man avowedly no friend to Government at the time, who got a pension without asking for it."

A few years after the publication of the Dictionary Tobias Smollett, the novelist, had referred to Johnson as "the great Cham of literature." The title was adapted from that of the fierce chiefs of the Tartars, and it suits Johnson well enough. He held the foremost place in the literary society of his day and in taverns and great men's halls alike could proclaim his opinions on literature and art, history and politics, morality and religion to men who, though "eminent in their departments," regarded it as an honour to be allowed to listen to him.

Lord Chesterfield, half in jest and half in earnest, had conferred on him the powers of a literary "dictator." The king's pension enabled Johnson to use his powers in a way of which Chesterfield had not dreamed.

Henceforward we know him not as a poet or essayist or even as "the great Lexicographer," but simply as "Doctor Johnson[1]," the talker, the traveller, the true-born Englishman.

With the exception of some political pamphlets, an account of his Scottish tour, and a series of *Lives of the Poets*, he wrote little of importance after 1762, comparing himself to a soldier who has fought a good many campaigns and is not to be blamed for retiring to ease and tranquillity.

BOSWELL. 'But I wonder, Sir, you have not more pleasure in writing than in not writing.'

JOHNSON. 'Sir, you *may* wonder.'

Johnson's Household

SO far we have seen little of Johnson's domestic life. He was happiest in a club or a tavern and, in the early days of struggle, home was not much more for him than the place where he sat

---

[1] The degree of Doctor of Laws was conferred on him by the University of Oxford in 1765.

down to write for a living. In his garret, which he considered as his library, a visitor would find "about five or six Greek folios, a deal writing-desk, and a chair and a half. Johnson giving to his guest the entire seat, tottered himself on one with only three legs and one arm."

But the household which he gradually gathered round him was a remarkable one.

Of Mrs Johnson's life in London we do not know much; but Johnson, being slovenly in his habits and cantankerous about his food, was bound to have "little disagreements" with a tidy housewife.

"My wife" he told Mrs Thrale "had a particular reverence for cleanliness, and desired the praise of neatness in her dress and furniture, as many ladies do, till they become troublesome to their best friends, slaves to their own besoms, and only sigh for the hour of sweeping their husbands out of the house as dirt and useless lumber."

When asked whether he ever "huffed his wife about his dinner," he replied:

"So often that at last she called to me, and said, 'Nay, hold, Mr Johnson, and do not make a farce of thanking God for a dinner which in a few minutes you will protest not eatable.'"

Sometimes she would get tired of the dirt and poverty of Fleet Street and stay for a time at Hampstead; but she could appreciate her husband's work and of Johnson's fondness for "his dear Tetty" there can be no doubt.

She died in March 1752, when Johnson had

just finished the last number of *The Rambler* and was still in the middle of his labours on the Dictionary. Here is the letter he wrote on the following day to his friend, Dr Taylor:

"DEAR SIR,

Let me have your company and instruction. Do not live away from me. My distress is great.

Pray desire Mrs Taylor to inform me what mourning I should buy for my mother and Miss Porter[1], and bring a note in writing with you.

Remember me in your prayers, for vain is the help of man.

I am, dear Sir, &c.,
SAM. JOHNSON.

March 18, 1752."

"'Sir,' he said twenty-six years later 'I have known what it was to have a wife, and (in a solemn tender faultering tone) I have known what it is to *lose a wife.*—It had almost broke my heart.'"

Long before the pension had given him security Johnson had begun to make his home a refuge for the poor and lonely:

"Though Johnson's circumstances were at this time far from being easy, his humane and charitable disposition was constantly exerting itself. Mrs Anna Williams, daughter of a very ingenious Welsh physician, and a woman of more than ordinary talents and literature, having come to London in hopes of being cured of a cataract in

---

[1] His step-daughter.

both her eyes, which afterwards ended in total blindness, was kindly received as a constant visitor at his house while Mrs Johnson lived; and after her death, having come under his roof in order to have an operation upon her eyes performed with more comfort to her than in lodgings, she had an apartment from him during the rest of her life, at all times when he had a house."

From the accounts we have of Mrs Williams we cannot imagine her to have been an easy companion. Her blindness made her peevish and quarrelsome and we may wonder, with Boswell, at Johnson's patience with her. But she was a good talker and that was a great merit in Johnson's eyes. He made many efforts to brighten her life and increase her tiny income; Garrick was induced to give her a benefit performance and Mrs Montagu to provide her with a small pension.

"The truth is," says Boswell "that his humane consideration of the forlorn and indigent state in which this lady was left by her father, induced him to treat her with the utmost tenderness, and even to be desirous of procuring her amusement, so as sometimes to incommode many of his friends, by carrying her with him to their houses, where, from her manner of eating, in consequence of her blindness, she could not but offend the delicacy of persons of nice sensations."

But Boswell was a proud man when he was first invited to drink tea with her after dining out with Johnson. He knew that it was a sign of real intimacy.

"We went home to his house to tea. Mrs

Williams made it with sufficient dexterity, not-withstanding her blindness, though her manner of satisfying herself that the cups were full enough appeared to me a little aukward; for I fancied she put her finger down a certain way, till she felt the tea touch it[1]. In my first elation at being allowed the privilege of attending Dr Johnson at his late visits to this lady..., I willingly drank cup after cup."

Nor was the lady's dinner forgotten when Boswell and Johnson went off to their tavern:

"There was, on these occasions, a little circumstance of kind attention to Mrs Williams, which must not be omitted. Before coming out, and leaving her to dine alone, he gave her her choice of a chicken, a sweetbread, or any other little nice thing, which was carefully sent to her from the tavern, ready-drest."

Her death left Johnson very desolate.

"I have lost a companion," he wrote "to whom I have had recourse for domestick amusement for thirty years, and whose variety of knowledge never was exhausted....She left her little substance to a charity-school. She is, I hope, where there is neither darkness, nor want, nor sorrow."

About 1746 Johnson had made the acquaintance of another "humble friend," Mr Robert Levet.

"He was" says Boswell "an obscure practiser in

---

[1] Boswell afterwards found he was mistaken. Mrs Williams "had acquired such a niceness of touch, as to know, by the feeling on the outside of the cup, how near it was to being full."

physick amongst the lower people, his fees being sometimes very small sums, sometimes whatever provisions his patients could afford him; but of such extensive practice in that way, that Mrs Williams has told me, his walk was from Hounsditch to Marybone....Such was Johnson's predilection for him, and fanciful estimation of his moderate abilities, that I have heard him say he should not be satisfied, though attended by all the College of Physicians, unless he had Mr Levet with him. Ever since I was acquainted with Dr Johnson, and many years before, as I have been assured by those who knew him earlier, Mr Levet had an apartment in his house, or his chambers, and waited upon him every morning, through the whole course of his late and tedious breakfast. He was of a strange grotesque appearance, stiff and formal in his manner, and seldom said a word while any company was present."

But this "odd old surgeon" was poor and honest; and that, as Goldsmith said, was recommendation enough to Johnson, who never treated him as a dependent and indeed declared that "Levet was indebted to him for nothing more than houseroom, his share in a penny-loaf at breakfast, and now and then a dinner on a Sunday." The greatest honour which Johnson paid his old friend were the "pathetick verses" which he wrote at his death. Here we will quote two stanzas:

Well try'd through many a varying year
  See *Levett* to the grave descend;
Officious, innocent, sincere,
  Of every friendless name the friend.

His virtues walk'd their narrow round,
  Nor made a pause, nor left a void;
And sure the Eternal Master found
  His single talent well employ'd.

For five years towards the end of his life Johnson had a further addition to his household.

"On Friday, March 20, [1778]" says Boswell "I found him at his own house, sitting with Mrs Williams, and was informed that the room formerly allotted to me was now appropriated to a charitable purpose; Mrs Desmoulins[1], and I think her daughter, and a Miss Carmichael, being all lodged in it. Such was his humanity, and such his generosity, that Mrs Desmoulins herself told me, he allowed her half-a-guinea a week. Let it be remembered, that this was above a twelfth part of his pension."

The invasion had, as we shall see, a disturbing effect on the household and it was well that Johnson had a devoted servant.

This was Francis Barber, a negro who had been brought to England in 1750 and received his freedom (for the slave trade still flourished) from his master, Colonel Bathurst. Dr Bathurst, the Colonel's son, was a very intimate friend of Johnson and gave him Francis as a servant. Johnson, as his way was, made of him a friend. Francis once took a fancy to go to sea; but Johnson had a horror of the sailor's life and got him back. Finding him intelligent and worth a better education he sent him to school at Bishop Stortford.

Here are two letters which shew Johnson's fatherly kindness:

[1] She was the daughter of Johnson's godfather.

"To Mr Francis Barber.

Dear Francis,

I have been very much out of order.
I am glad to hear that you are well, and design
to come soon to see you. I would have you stay
at Mrs Clapp's for the present, till I can deter-
mine what we shall do. Be a good boy.

My compliments to Mrs Clapp and to Mr
Fowler. I am,

Your's affectionately,

Sam. Johnson.

May 28, 1768."

"To Mr Francis Barber, at Mrs Clapp's,
Bishop-Stortford, Hertfordshire.

Dear Francis,

I am at last sat down to write to you,
and should very much blame myself for having
neglected you so long, if I did not impute that
and many other failings to want of health. I hope
not to be so long silent again. I am very well
satisfied with your progress, if you can really
perform the exercises which you are set....

Let me know what English books you read for
your entertainment. You can never be wise unless you love reading.

Do not imagine that I shall forget or forsake
you ; for if, when I examine you, I find that you
have not lost your time, you shall want no encouragement from

Yours affectionately,

Sam. Johnson.

London, Sept. 25, 1770."

After his four years' schooling Francis returned to London and remained a faithful servant till his master's death. When Johnson was making his will he "asked Dr Brocklesby what would be a proper annuity to a favourite servant, and being answered that it must depend on the circumstances of the master; and, that in the case of a nobleman, fifty pounds a year was considered as an adequate reward for many years' faithful service; 'Then (said Johnson,) shall I be *nobilissimus*, for I mean to leave Frank seventy pounds a year, and I desire you to tell him so.'"

Lastly, we must mention a fireside creature that Johnson loved:

"I shall never forget" says Boswell "the indulgence with which he treated Hodge, his cat: for whom he himself used to go out and buy oysters, lest the servants having that trouble should take a dislike to the poor creature. I am, unluckily, one of those who have an antipathy to a cat, so that I am uneasy when in the room with one; and I own, I frequently suffered a good deal from the presence of this same Hodge. I recollect him one day scrambling up Dr Johnson's breast, apparently with much satisfaction, while my friend smiling and half-whistling, rubbed down his back, and pulled him by the tail; and when I observed he was a fine cat, saying, 'Why yes, Sir, but I have had cats whom I liked better than this'; and then as if perceiving Hodge to be out of countenance, adding, 'but he is a very fine cat, a very fine cat indeed.'"

How did this "crowd of wretched old creatures," as Macaulay rather unkindly calls them, agree? Not very well. Hodge was probably the only peaceful member.

In 1778 the following conversation took place between Johnson and his friends Mr and Mrs Thrale:

"MRS THRALE. Pray, Sir, how does Mrs Williams like all this tribe? DR JOHNSON. Madam, she does not like them at all; but their fondness for her is not greater. She and Desmoulins quarrel incessantly.... MR THRALE. And pray who is clerk of your kitchen, Sir? DR JOHNSON. Why, Sir, I am afraid there is none; a general anarchy prevails in my kitchen, as I am told by Mr Levett, who says it is not now what it used to be. MRS THRALE. Mr Levett, I suppose, Sir, has the office of keeping the hospital in health, for he is an apothecary. DR JOHNSON. Levett, Madam, is a brutal fellow, but I have a good regard for him; for his brutality is in his manners, not his mind. MR THRALE. But how do you get your dinners drest? DR JOHNSON. Why, Desmoulins has the chief management of the kitchen; but our roasting is not magnificent, for we have no jack. MR THRALE. No jack! Why, how do they manage without? DR JOHNSON. Small joints, I believe, they manage with a string, and larger are done at the tavern.... MRS THRALE. But pray, Sir, who is the Poll[1] you talk of? She that you used to abet in her quarrels with Mrs Williams, and call out, *At her again, Poll! Never flinch, Poll!*

[1] Poll was Miss Carmichael. See page 49.

DR JOHNSON. Why, I took to Poll very well at first, but she won't do upon a nearer examination.
MRS THRALE. How came she among you, Sir?
DR JOHNSON. Why I don't rightly remember, but we could spare her very well from us. Poll is a stupid slut. I had some hopes of her at first; but when I talked to her tightly and closely, I could make nothing of her; she was wiggle waggle...."

Nothing, perhaps, makes us realise more fully Johnson's largeness of heart than the picture of his extraordinary household.

Goldsmith was right when he said: "Johnson, to be sure, has a roughness in his manner; but no man alive has a more tender heart. *He has nothing of the bear but his skin.*"

His daily Life

JOHNSON could tolerate the quarrels of his household and the anarchy of his kitchen better than most men, for the simple reason that he generally dined out at about 2 o'clock and stayed in a club or a tavern or a friend's house until bedtime. A tavern chair was for him "the throne of human felicity" and we shall shortly see him as he loved best to be—"folding his legs and having his talk out" with his friends.

First, let us see something of his daily habits

and manner of life. Here is Boswell's description
of him in later years :

"His person was large, robust, I may say ap-
proaching to the gigantick, and grown unwieldy
from corpulency. His countenance was naturally
of the cast of an ancient statue, but somewhat disfigured by the scars of that *evil*, which, it was
formerly imagined, the *royal touch* could cure. He
was now...become a little dull of hearing. His
sight had always been somewhat weak ; yet, so
much does mind govern, and even supply the
deficiency of organs, that his perceptions were
uncommonly quick and accurate. His head, and
sometime also his body shook with a kind of
motion like the effect of a palsy : he appeared
to be frequently disturbed by cramps, or convulsive contractions, of the nature of that distemper
called *St Vitus's dance*. He wore a full suit of plain
brown clothes, with twisted hair-buttons of the
same colour, a large bushy greyish wig, a plain
shirt, black worsted stockings, and silver buckles."

His day began late with a breakfast consisting
of a penny-loaf and a large pot of tea. It was not
usually a very tidy meal, for Johnson often appeared "in deshabille, as just risen from bed";
Levet poured out the tea, while Johnson clumsily
divided the bread.

When there was a guest, however, his "tea and
rolls and butter, and whole breakfast apparatus
were all in such decorum, and his behaviour was
so courteous" that the visitor "was quite surprised, and wondered at his having heard so much
said of Johnson's slovenliness and roughness."

Once, when Boswell called unexpectedly before he was up, he called briskly "Frank, go and get coffee, and let us breakfast *in splendour.*"

But these splendid occasions were exceptional.

"About twelve o'clock" wrote Dr Maxwell, a 'social friend' of Johnson, "I commonly visited him, and frequently found him in bed, or declaiming over his tea, which he drank very plentifully. He generally had a levee of morning visitors, chiefly men of letters; Hawkesworth, Goldsmith, Murphy, Langton, Steevens, Beauclerk &c. &c., and sometimes learned ladies, particularly I remember a French lady of wit and fashion doing him the honour of a visit. He seemed to be considered as a kind of publick oracle, whom every body thought they had a right to visit and consult; and doubtless they were well rewarded. I never could discover how he found time for his compositions. He declaimed all the morning, then went to dinner at a tavern, where he commonly staid late, and then drank his tea at some friend's house, over which he loitered a great while, but seldom took supper. I fancy he must have read and wrote chiefly in the night, for I can scarcely recollect that he ever refused going with me to a tavern, and he often went to Ranelagh, which he deemed a place of innocent recreation. He frequently gave all the silver in his pocket to the poor, who watched him, between his house and the tavern where he dined. He walked the streets at all hours and said he was never robbed, for the rogues knew he had little money, nor had the appearance of having much."

Such was Johnson's week-day life. Sunday was another matter.

"It should be different (he observed) from another day. People may walk, but not throw stones at birds. There may be relaxation, but there should be no levity."

He made some good resolutions accordingly:

"To rise early, and in order to it, to go sleep early on Saturday....

To read the Scripture methodically....

To go to church twice.

To read books of Divinity....

To wear off by meditation any worldly soil contracted in the week."

As he himself confessed, he did not always keep his resolutions, but that religion was a real part of Johnson's life and work is shewn not only by a score of incidents and conversations recorded by Boswell, but by the numerous *Prayers and Meditations* which were collected and published after his death. This was his prayer as he began the second volume of the Dictionary:

"O GOD, who hast hitherto supported me, enable me to proceed in this labour, and in the whole task of my present state; that when I shall render up, at the last day, an account of the talent committed to me, I may receive pardon, for the sake of JESUS CHRIST. Amen."

His favourite place of worship was St Clement Danes and in the churchyard to-day we may see his figure facing the street he loved best and still seeming ready to "defend the most minute circumstance connected with the Church of England."

Partly from ill-health, partly by natural disposition, Johnson was incurably lazy.

"I have been trying" he told Boswell "to cure my laziness all my life, and could not do it."

He slept badly and had no inclination to go to bed; indeed he seldom came home till two in the morning. Nor, as we shall see[1], did he mind being roused in the middle of the night, if there was some fun to be had.

"He has more fun" said his friend Miss Burney "and comical humour and love of nonsense about him than almost anybody I ever saw."

His laugh was "a kind of good humoured growl" or, as Tom Davies the bookseller described it, "he laughed like a rhinoceros."

Boswell could not always share this boisterous amusement and was puzzled at his hero being "exceedingly diverted at what seemed to others a very small sport."

One evening they were sitting in the Temple with a lawyer named Chambers who had just been drawing up a will for Johnson's friend, Langton. Johnson's sense of humour was for some reason keenly tickled by this; he twitted Chambers with having made the will himself and ran on in a playful manner, "which certainly was not such as might be expected from the authour of *The Rambler*."

"Ha, ha, ha!" he bellowed "I hope he has left

[1] See page 113.

me a legacy. I'd have his will turned into verse,
like a ballad."

In the street, " Johnson could not stop his merriment, but continued it all the way till we got without the Temple-gate. He then burst into such a
fit of laughter, that he appeared to be almost in
a convulsion ; and, in order to support himself,
laid hold of one of the posts at the side of the
foot pavement, and sent forth peals so loud, that
in the silence of the night his voice seemed to re-
sound from Temple-bar to Fleet-ditch."

Poor Boswell is almost ashamed to record what
he calls "this most ludicrous exhibition of the
aweful, melancholy, and venerable Johnson,"
but most of his readers prefer this picture of
Johnson staggering in helpless laughter down
Fleet Street to the most impressive essay in
The Rambler.

Johnson's oddities in the street must often
have made people turn round to look at him. He
always took care, for instance, "to go out or in at
a door or passage by a certain number of steps
from a certain point, or at least so as that either
his right or his left foot, (I am not certain which,)
should constantly make the first actual movement
when he came close to the door or passage. Thus
I conjecture : for I have, upon innumerable occasions, observed him suddenly stop, and then seem
to count his steps with a deep earnestness ; and
when he had neglected or gone wrong in this sort
of magical movement, I have seen him go back
again, put himself in a proper posture to begin the
ceremony, and, having gone through it, break

from his abstraction, walk briskly on, and join his companion."

He was full of these childish tricks. He would never, if he could help it, step on the cracks between paving-stones; when passing a row of posts, he was careful to touch the top of each with his hand; and all the time he would probably be talking to himself and jerking his head and limbs in the queer way which was habitual with him.

Indoors he was the same. Strangers could not make him out:

"Johnson used to be a pretty frequent visitor at the house of Mr Richardson, authour of *Clarissa*, and other novels of extensive reputation. Mr Hogarth came one day to see Richardson, soon after the execution of Dr Cameron, for having taken arms for the house of Stuart in 1745–6."

Hogarth was "a warm partisan of George the Second" and defended the king's decision.

"While he was talking, he perceived a person standing at a window in the room, shaking his head, and rolling himself about in a strange ridiculous manner. He concluded that he was an ideot, whom his relations had put under the care of Mr Richardson, as a very good man. To his great surprize, however, this figure stalked forwards to where he and Mr Richardson were sitting, and all at once took up the argument, and burst out into an invective against George the Second, as one, who, upon all occasions, was unrelenting and barbarous....He displayed such a power of eloquence, that Hogarth looked at him with astonishment, and actually imagined that this ideot had been at the moment

inspired. Neither Hogarth nor Johnson were
made known to each other at this interview."

It is a pity Hogarth has not left us a picture of
the scene.

Although he never wished to have a child of his
own, Johnson had a warm corner in his heart for
young people:

"Mr Strahan [the printer] had taken a poor boy
from the country as an apprentice, upon Johnson's
recommendation. Johnson having enquired after
him, said, 'Mr Strahan, let me have five guineas
on account, and I'll give this boy one. Nay, if a
man recommends a boy, and does nothing for him,
it is sad work. Call him down.' I followed him
into the court-yard, behind Mr Strahan's house....
'Well, my boy, how do you go on?'–'Pretty well,
Sir; but they are afraid I an't strong enough for
some parts of the business.' JOHNSON. 'Why, I
shall be sorry for it; for when you consider with
how little mental power and corporeal labour a
printer can get a guinea a week, it is a very desir-
able occupation for you. Do you hear,—take all
the pains you can; and if this does not do, we must
think of some other way of life for you. There's
a guinea.'"

To his friends' children he liked to appear as a
benevolent great-uncle; when Mrs Thrale was
away from home, he would send her reports from
the nursery:

"I went this afternoon to visit the two babies at
Kensington, and found them indeed a little spotted
with their disorder, but as brisk and gay as health

and youth can make them. I took a paper of sweet-meats and spread them on the table. They took great delight to shew their governess the various animals that were made of sugar; and when they had eaten as much as was fit, the rest were laid up for to-morrow."

Here is another letter written in his seventy-fifth year—seven months before his death:

"To Miss Jane Langton.

May 10, 1784.

My Dearest Miss Jenny,

I am sorry that your pretty letter has been so long without being answered; but, when I am not pretty well, I do not always write plain enough for young ladies. I am glad, my dear, to see that you write so well, and hope that you mind your pen, your book, and your needle, for they are all necessary. Your books will give you know-ledge, and make you respected; and your needle will find you useful employment when you do not care to read. When you are a little older, I hope you will be very diligent in learning arithmetick; and, above all, that through your whole life you will carefully say your prayers, and read your Bible.

I am, my dear, your most humble servant,

SAM. JOHNSON."

"He must have been a bold laugher," says Boswell "who would have ventured to tell Dr Johnson of any of his particularities."

But when a little girl asked him "Pray, Dr Johnson, why do you make such strange gestures?"

"From bad habit" he replied. "Do you, my dear, take care to guard against bad habits."

Had the questioner been some distinguished man, the reply would more likely have been: "Why, Sir, because I choose to, and there's an end on't."

His Clubs

IN spite of his oddities, Johnson was, before everything, a social man. The great business of his life, he said, was to escape from himself, and he would never trust himself alone, "but when employed in writing or reading." He would beg a friend to go home with him simply to avoid being alone in the coach.

"It was a very remarkable circumstance about Johnson, whom shallow observers have supposed to have been ignorant of the world, that very few men had seen greater variety of characters.... The suddenness with which his accounts of some of them started out in conversation, was not less pleasing than surprising. I remember he once observed to me, 'It is wonderful, Sir, what is to be found in London. The most literary conversation that I ever enjoyed, was at the table of Jack Ellis, a money-scrivener behind the Royal Exchange, with whom I at one period used to dine generally once a week.'

Volumes would be required to contain a list of his numerous and various acquaintance, none of whom he ever forgot....He associated with persons the most widely different in manners, abilities, rank and accomplishments. He was at once the companion of the brilliant Colonel Forrester of the Guards...and of the aukward and uncouth Robert Levet; of Lord Thurlow[1], and Mr Sastres, the Italian master; and has dined one day with the beautiful, gay, and fascinating Lady Craven, and the next with good Mrs Gardiner, the tallow-chandler, on Snow-hill."

In the company of "social friends" Johnson found his greatest pleasure. His own definition of a club was: "An assembly of good fellows, meeting under certain conditions," and it is characteristic of him that he was the inventor of the word *clubable*.

For, in Johnson's day, clubs were not luxurious halls where conversation was carried on in under-tones; vigorous talking (with some eating and drinking) was the chief object of the company that gathered round the tavern table.

Of Johnson's talk we need not say much here. It was, and is, his chief title to fame. In his life-time a roomful of people would wait in expectant silence for him to begin; to-day his conversation remains the chief attraction of Boswell's *Life* and of the many other books, great and small, that have been written about him.

Johnson looked upon conversation as a serious art and said that a good talker should have know-

[1] The Lord Chancellor.

ledge, command of words, imagination and a resolution not to be overcome by failures.   This last
he considered essential; and he certainly was not
often overcome himself, for he could not bear to
be worsted in argument, "even when he had taken
the wrong side." Hence his habit of "talking for
victory."

But Johnson could not talk his best if the dinner
had not been good. "For my part," he said in his
blunt way "I mind my belly very studiously, and
very carefully."

"I never knew any man" says Boswell "who
relished good eating more than he did. When at
table, he was totally absorbed in the business of the
moment; his looks seemed rivetted to his plate;
nor would he, unless when in very high company,
say one word, or even pay the least attention to
what was said by others, till he had satisfied his
appetite, which was so fierce, and indulged with
such intenseness, that while in the act of eating,
the veins of his forehead swelled, and generally a
strong perspiration was visible. To those whose
sensations were delicate, this could not but be dis-
gusting....It must be owned that Johnson, though
he could be rigidly *abstemious*, was not a *temperate*
man either in eating or drinking. He could refrain, but he could not use moderately."

Johnson realised this well enough. So from 1736
to 1757 and for the last twenty years of his life he
drank no wine at all[1], except on special occasions.
Once or twice he persuaded Boswell also to be "a
water-drinker, upon trial"; but it is to be feared

[1] See page 108.

that Boswell found it as hard to refrain as to use moderately—he had many a morning headache.

Wine or no wine, Johnson saw no reason why he should be abstemious over the tea-cups. In a famous review of an *Essay on Tea* he described himself as "a hardened and shameless tea-drinker, who has for twenty years diluted his meals with only the infusion of this fascinating plant; whose kettle has scarcely time to cool; who with tea amuses the evening, with tea solaces the midnight, and with tea welcomes the morning."

After pouring out his sixteenth cup, a hostess once asked him if a small basin would not save him trouble. "'I wonder, Madam,' answered he roughly, 'why all the ladies ask me such questions. It is to save yourselves trouble, Madam, and not me.' The lady was silent and resumed her task."

Johnson founded his first club, as we have seen, as a relief from his monotonous work on the Dictionary. It was a small society which met once a week at the King's Head, "a famous beef-steak house" in Ivy Lane.

"Thither" wrote a member of the club "he constantly resorted with a disposition to please and be pleased. Our conversations seldom began till after a supper so very solid and substantial as led us to think that with him it was a dinner... his habitual melancholy and lassitude of spirit gave way; his countenance brightened."

The Ivy Lane club broke up after about eight years, but some months before his death Johnson "had the pleasure of giving another dinner to the remainder of the old club." "We were as cheerful," he wrote, "as in former times; only I could not make quite so much noise."

Towards the end of his life, too, he formed the Essex Head Club, of which "the terms were lax and the expenses light." It had some distinguished members and Boswell has preserved an interesting set of rules as drafted by Johnson; but by far the most famous of Johnson's clubs was the society known as The Literary Club, founded in 1764.

"Sir Joshua Reynolds had the merit of being the first proposer of it, to which Johnson acceded, and the original members were, Sir Joshua Reynolds, Dr Johnson, Mr Edmund Burke, Dr Nugent, Mr Beauclerk, Mr Langton, Dr Goldsmith, Mr Chamier, and Sir John Hawkins. They met at the Turk's Head, in Gerrard-street, Soho, one evening in every week, at seven, and generally continued their conversation till a pretty late hour. This club has been gradually increased to its present number, thirty-five."

Johnson did not at first encourage an increase in the number of members:

"Dr Goldsmith said once to Dr Johnson, that he wished for some additional members to the LITERARY CLUB, to give it an agreeable variety; for (said he) there can now be nothing new among us: we have travelled over one another's minds. Johnson seemed a little angry, and said, 'Sir, you have not travelled over *my* mind, I promise you.'"

Boswell gives us a list of members in a later

year. In it we find the names of Adam Smith, the political economist, Gibbon the historian, Fox the politician, Sir Joseph Banks the explorer, Sheridan the dramatist, Garrick the actor, and a number of bishops, statesmen, doctors and law-yers—all men of distinction; and over them all towered the figure, and afterwards the memory, of Samuel Johnson.

Boswell does not record many accounts of con-versations at the Club. Probably the rules did not allow him to repeat much of what was said there. But here are one or two extracts:

"JOHNSON. 'I have been reading Thicknesse's *Travels*, which I think are entertaining.' BOSWELL. 'What, Sir, a good book?' JOHNSON. 'Yes, Sir, to read once; I do not say you are to make a study of it, and digest it; and I believe it to be a true book in his intention. All travellers generally mean to tell truth....''

"E.[1] From the experience which I have had,—and I have had a great deal,—I have learnt to think *better* of mankind.' JOHNSON. 'From my experi-ence I have found them worse in commercial dealings, more disposed to cheat, than I had any notion of; but more disposed to do one another good than I had conceived...and really it is won-derful, considering how much attention is neces-sary for men to take care of themselves, and ward off immediate evils which press upon them, it is wonderful how much they do for others. As it is said of the greatest liar, that he tells more truth than falsehood; so it may be said of the worst

[1] No doubt Edmund Burke.

man, that he does more good than evil.' Boswell.
'Perhaps from experience men may be found
happier than we suppose.' Johnson. 'No, Sir;
the more we enquire, we shall find men the less
happy....'

"Boswell. 'I have known a man resolved to
put friendship to the test, by asking a friend to
lend him money merely with that view, when he
did not want it.' Johnson. 'That is very wrong,
Sir. Your friend may be a narrow man, and yet
have many good qualities : narrowness may be his
only fault. Now you are trying his general character as a friend, by one particular singly, in which
he happens to be defective, when, in truth, his
character is composed of many particulars.'"

"E. 'I understand the hogshead of claret,
which this society was favoured with by our
friend the Dean, is nearly out; I think he should
be written to, to send another of the same kind...'
Johnson. 'I am willing to offer my services as
secretary on this occasion.' P. 'As many as are
for Dr Johnson being secretary hold up your
hands.—Carried unanimously.' Boswell. 'He
will be our Dictator.' Johnson. 'No, the company is to dictate to me....'"

Boswell seldom had the last word. At another
meeting of the Club :

"One of the company[1] attempted, with too
much forwardness, to rally him on his late appearance at the theatre; but had reason to repent of
his temerity. 'Why, Sir, did you go to Mrs Abing-
ton's[2] benefit ? Did you see ?' Johnson. 'No, Sir.'

[1] Probably Boswell.   [2] A famous actress.

'Did you hear?' JOHNSON. 'No, Sir.' 'Why then, Sir, did you go?' JOHNSON. 'Because, Sir, she is a favourite of the publick; and when the publick cares the thousandth part for you that it does for her, I will go to your benefit too.'"

It was on the day after this meeting that Boswell tried, in vain, to solve the mystery of one of Johnson's oddities:

"Next morning I won a small bet from Lady Diana Beauclerk, by asking him as to one of his particularities, which her Ladyship laid I durst not do. It seems he had been frequently observed at the Club to put into his pocket the Seville oranges, after he had squeezed the juice of them into the drink which he made for himself. Beauclerk and Garrick talked of it to me, and seemed to think that he had a strange unwillingness to be discovered. We could not divine what he did with them; and this was the bold question to be put. I saw on his table the spoils of the preceding night, some fresh peels nicely scraped and cut into pieces. 'O, Sir, (said I) I now partly see what you do with the squeezed oranges which you put into your pocket at the Club.' JOHNSON. 'I have a great love for them.' BOSWELL. 'And pray, Sir, what do you do with them? You scrape them, it seems, very neatly, and what next?' JOHNSON. 'Let them dry, Sir.' BOSWELL. 'And what next?' JOHNSON. 'Nay, Sir, you shall know their fate no further.' BOSWELL. 'Then the world must be left in the dark. It must be said (assuming a mock solemnity,) he scraped them, and let them dry, but what he did with them next, he never could be prevailed upon to tell.'

JOHNSON. 'Nay, Sir, you should say it more em-
phatically:—he could not be prevailed upon, even
by his dearest friends, to tell.'"

And to this day the world can only conjecture.

Enter Boswell

BOSWELL and many others of Johnson's
friends have already entered so often into
the foregoing pages, that it is time we gave some
space to the more prominent members of
Johnson's circle.

James Boswell was more than thirty years
younger than Johnson, being born at Edinburgh
in 1740. He was the son of a Scottish judge, Lord
Auchinleck, and his own inclination was to be an
officer in the Guards; but at his father's wish he
entered the profession of the law, and studied, not
very industriously, first at Edinburgh and afterwards at Glasgow University. He dabbled in
poetry and literary criticism and longed for the
gayer world and more cultured society of London.
He first visited the capital in 1760 and on his
second visit fulfilled what was then the greatest
ambition of his life—he met Dr Johnson.

Boswell's account of this meeting has become
one of the most famous passages in English literature and part of it, at any rate, must be repeated
here:

JAMES BOSWELL

"Mr Thomas Davies the actor, who then kept a bookseller's shop in Russel-street, Covent-garden, told me that Johnson was very much his friend, and came frequently to his house, where he more than once invited me to meet him; but by some unlucky accident or other he was prevented from coming to us. Mr Thomas Davies was a man of good understanding and talents, with the advantage of a liberal education....[He] recollected several of Johnson's remarkable sayings, and was one of the best of the many imitators of his voice and manner, while relating them. He increased my impatience more and more to see the extraordinary man whose works I highly valued, and whose conversation was reported to be so peculiarly excellent. At last, on Monday the 16th of May [1763], when I was sitting in Mr Davies's back-parlour, after having drunk tea with him and Mrs Davies, Johnson unexpectedly came into the shop; and Mr Davies having perceived him through the glass-door in the room in which we were sitting, advancing towards us,—he announced his aweful approach to me, somewhat in the manner of an actor in the part of Horatio, when he addresses Hamlet on the appearance of his father's ghost, 'Look, my Lord, it comes.' I found that I had a very perfect idea of Johnson's figure, from the portrait of him painted by Sir Joshua Reynolds soon after he had published his *Dictionary*, in the attitude of sitting in his easy chair in deep meditation, which was the first picture his friend did for him....Mr Davies mentioned my name, and respectfully introduced me to him. I was much agitated; and recollecting his prejudice against the Scotch, of which I had heard much, I said to Davies, 'Don't tell where I come from.'—'From Scotland,' cried Davies roguishly. 'Mr Johnson, (said I) I do indeed come from Scotland, but I cannot help it.' I am willing to flatter myself that I meant this as light pleasantry to sooth and conciliate him, and not as an humiliating abasement at the expence of my country. But however that might be, this speech was somewhat unlucky; for with that quickness of wit for which he was so remarkable, he seized the expression 'come from Scotland,' which I used in the sense of being of that country; and, as if I had said that I had come away from it, or left it, retorted, 'That, Sir, I find, is what a very great many of your countrymen cannot help.' This stroke stunned me a good deal; and when we had sat down, I felt myself not a little embarrassed, and apprehensive of what might come next. He then addressed himself to Davies: 'What do you think of Garrick? He has refused me an order for the play for Miss Williams, because he knows the house will be full, and that an order would be worth three shillings.' Eager to take any opening to get into conversation with him, I ventured to say, 'O, Sir, I cannot think Mr Garrick would grudge such a trifle to you.' 'Sir (said he, with a stern look,) I have known David Garrick longer than you have done: and I know no right you have to talk to me on the subject.' Perhaps I deserved this check; for it was rather presumptuous in me, an entire stranger, to express any doubt of the justice of his animadversion upon his old acquaintance and pupil. I now felt myself much mortified, and began to think that the hope which I had long indulged of obtaining his acquaintance was blasted. And, in truth, had not my ardour been uncommonly strong, and my resolution uncommonly persevering, so rough a reception might have deterred me for ever from making any further attempts. Fortunately, however, I remained upon the field not wholly discomfited; and was soon rewarded by hearing some of his conversation...."

Before the end of the interview Boswell recovered a little from his nervousness; but, as he was going, complained to Davies of the hard blows the great man had given him. Davies, who had no doubt enjoyed the evening with considerable relish, cheered him by saying "Don't be uneasy. I can see he likes you very well."

A few days later Boswell made a further venture. He "boldly repaired" to Johnson's chambers on the first floor on No. 1 Inner-Temple-lane.

"He received me very courteously; but it must be confessed, that his apartment, and furniture, and morning dress, were sufficiently uncouth. His brown suit of cloaths looked very rusty; he had on a little old shrivelled unpowdered wig, which was too small for his head; his shirt-neck and knees of his breeches were loose; his black worsted stockings ill drawn up; and he had a pair of unbuckled shoes by way of slippers. But all these slovenly particularities were forgotten the moment that he began to talk. Some gentlemen, whom I do not recollect, were sitting with him; and when they went away, I also rose; but he said to me, 'Nay, don't go.' 'Sir (said I,) I am afraid that I intrude upon you. It is benevolent to allow me to sit and hear you.' He seemed pleased with this compliment, which I sincerely paid him, and answered, 'Sir, I am obliged to any man who visits me.'"

He soon reached a further stage of intimacy:

"I had learnt that his place of frequent resort was the Mitre tavern in Fleet-street, where he loved to sit up late, and I begged I might be allowed to pass an evening with him there soon, which he promised I should. A few days afterwards I met him near Temple-bar, about one o'clock in the morning, and asked him if he would then go to the Mitre. 'Sir, (said he) it is too late; they won't let us in. But I'll go with you another night with all my heart.'"

There is only one way to follow the progress of this friendship—and that is to read Boswell's own story of it.

Boswell did not get on very happily with his father and, whenever he could, left his highland home for London; and in London his chief delight was to be with Johnson. They often travelled together and in a later chapter we shall read some account of their journeys, especially of Johnson's visit to Scotland, about which each of them wrote a book.

Here we will be content with a few typical incidents and conversations in the long friendship.

Johnson could not have found a better listener than "Bozzy," as he soon began to call him. Boswell's worship of his hero may often seem to us absurd, but we may be sure that Johnson would never have tolerated, much less loved, a man who was simply a flatterer.

Boswell was really interested in the things Johnson talked about and, without any pretence, enjoyed the same kind of pleasures—dining out, arguing over a good bottle of port, staying at friends' houses, examining cathedrals, wandering up and down Fleet Street, coming down late to breakfast. "No man," as Johnson said, "is a hypocrite in his pleasures."

Moreover, Johnson "loved the acquaintance of young people."

"Sir," he said "young men have more virtue than old men; they have more generous sentiments in every respect. I love the young dogs of this age: they have more wit and humour and knowledge of life than we had; but then the dogs are not so good scholars."

Boswell was certainly "a young dog"; and even the fact that he came from Scotland must have been a source of pleasure to Johnson, who, when he had no other retort ready, could always bring out the old joke in a new form.

Above all, Boswell was *clubable*; and Johnson could give no higher praise.

But we must return to the Mitre, where Boswell is now a proud host:

"I had as my guests this evening at the Mitre tavern, Dr Johnson, Dr Goldsmith, Mr Thomas Davies, Mr Eccles...and the Reverend Mr John Ogilvie, who was desirous of being in company

with my illustrious friend, while I, in my turn,
was proud to have the honour of shewing one of
my countrymen upon what easy terms Johnson
permitted me to live with him…Mr Ogilvie was
unlucky enough to choose for the topick of his
conversation the praises of his native country. He
began with saying, that there was very rich land
round Edinburgh. Goldsmith, who had studied
physick there, contradicted this, very untruly,
with a sneering laugh. Disconcerted a little by
this, Mr Ogilvie then took new ground, where, I
suppose, he thought himself perfectly safe ; for he
observed, that Scotland had a great many noble
wild prospects. JOHNSON. 'I believe, Sir, you have
a great many. Norway, too, has noble wild prospects ; and Lapland is remarkable for prodigious
noble wild prospects. But, Sir, let me tell you,
the noblest prospect which a Scotchman ever sees,
is the high road that leads him to England !'"

The friendship ripened quickly. When Boswell announced that he would shortly be going to
Utrecht to continue his study of the law, Johnson
said, "I must see thee out of England ; I will accompany you to Harwich." Boswell "could not
find words to express what he felt upon this un-
expected and very great mark of his affectionate
regard."

When the time came, he was loth to go :

"After tea he carried me to what he called his
walk, which was a long narrow paved court in the
neighbourhood, overshadowed by some trees.
There we sauntered a considerable time ; and I
complained to him that my love of London and

of his company was such, that I shrunk almost from the thought of going away, even to travel, which is generally so much desired by young men. He roused me by manly and spirited conversation. He advised me, when settled in any place abroad, to study with an eagerness after knowledge and to apply to Greek an hour every day; and when I was moving about, to read diligently the great book of mankind."

On the way to Harwich Johnson was more jocular. In the stage coach "a fat elderly gentle-woman, and a young Dutchman seemed the most inclined among us to conversation. At the inn where we dined, the gentlewoman said that she had done her best to educate her children; and particularly that she had never suffered them to be a moment idle. JOHNSON. 'I wish, Madam, you would educate me too; for I have been an idle fellow all my life.' 'I am sure, Sir, (said she) you have not been idle.' JOHNSON. 'Nay, Madam, it is very true; and that gentleman there (pointing to me,) has been idle. He was idle at Edinburgh. His father sent him to Glasgow, where he continued to be idle. He then came to London, where he has been very idle; and now he is going to Utrecht, where he will be as idle as ever.' I asked him privately how he could expose me so. JOHNSON. 'Poh, poh! (said he) they knew nothing about you, and will think of it no more.'"

The first meeting between these two men had taken place in May 1763. Boswell left for Utrecht in the August of the same year. His description of his farewell to Johnson at Harwich shews how firmly their friendship had been formed in a few months :

"My revered friend walked down with me to the beach, where we embraced and parted with tenderness, and engaged to correspond by letters. I said, 'I hope, Sir, you will not forget me in my absence.' JOHNSON. 'Nay, Sir, it is more likely you should forget me, than that I should forget you.' As the vessel put out to sea, I kept my eyes upon him for a considerable time, while he remained rolling his majestick frame in his usual manner : and at last I perceived him walk back into the town, and he disappeared."

More about Boswell .

BOSWELL travelled a good deal and visited several European countries besides Holland. He took a special interest in Corsica and afterwards wrote a book about the people of the island. Johnson was at first discouraging on this subject and wished Boswell would empty his head of it, but he afterwards highly praised his *Journal.*

On his return to London, Boswell found that his admiration of his hero's "extraordinary mind" was "increased and confirmed," and when, a few years later, he was about to be married, he promised himself a great deal of instructive conversation with Johnson "on the conduct of the married state," but Johnson (who said once that marriages in general would be as happy, and often more so, if they were all made by the Lord Chancellor) "did not say much upon that topick."

When Johnson went to stay with his friend in Scotland, Mrs Boswell found his visit quite long enough :

"The truth is, that his irregular hours and uncouth habits, such as turning the candles with their heads downwards, when they did not burn bright enough, and letting the wax drop upon the carpet, could not but be disagreeable to a lady. Besides, she had not that high admiration of him which was felt by most of those who knew him ; and what was very natural to a female mind, she thought he had too much influence over her husband. She once in a little warmth, made, with more point than justice, this remark upon that subject: 'I have seen many a bear led by a man ; but I never before saw a man led by a bear.'"

It is delightful to note Boswell's pride as each fresh link is formed in the chain of friendship. Johnson, as we have seen, was a devout Christian and encouraged his friend to join him in his devotions :

"On the 9th of April [1773], being Good Friday, I breakfasted with him on tea and cross-buns; *Doctor* Levet, as Frank called him, making the tea. He carried me with him to the Church of St Clement Danes, where he had his seat; and his behaviour was, as I had imaged to myself, solemnly devout. I never shall forget the tremulous earnestness with which he pronounced the awful petition in the Litany: 'In the hour of death, and at the day of judgement, good LORD deliver us.' We went to church both in the morning and evening. In the interval between the two services we did not dine; but he read in the Greek New Testament, and I turned over several of his books."

Two days later he had his first dinner at Johnson's house:

"I had...great curiosity to dine with DR SAMUEL JOHNSON, in the dusky recess of a court in Fleet-street. I supposed we should scarcely have knives and forks, and only some strange, uncouth, ill-drest dish: but I found every thing in very good order. We had no other company but Mrs Williams and a young woman whom I did not know. As a dinner here was considered as a singular phænomenon, and as I was frequently interrogated on the subject, my readers may perhaps be desirous to know our bill of fare...We had a very good soup, a boiled leg of lamb and spinach, a veal pye, and a rice pudding."

Boswell was made still prouder when shortly afterwards he was admitted to the Club:

"On Friday, April 30, I dined with him at Mr Beauclerk's, where were Lord Charlemont, Sir Joshua Reynolds, and some more members of the LITERARY CLUB, whom he had obligingly invited to meet me, as I was this evening to be balloted for as candidate for admission into that distinguished society. Johnson had done me the honour to propose me, and Beauclerk was very zealous for me...."

"The gentlemen went away to their club, and I

was left at Beauclerk's till the fate of my election should be announced to me. I sat in a state of anxiety which even the charming conversation of Lady Di Beauclerk could not entirely dissipate. In a short time I received the agreeable intelligence that I was chosen. I hastened to the place of meeting, and was introduced to such a society as can seldom be found.... Upon my entrance, Johnson placed himself behind a chair, on which he leaned as on a desk or pulpit, and with humorous formality gave me a *Charge,* pointing out the conduct expected from me as a good member of this club."

When they were travelling together in Scotland Johnson frankly told him a little more about the election, and Boswell as frankly tells us:

"He told me, 'Sir, you got into our club by doing what a man can do. Several of the members wished to keep you out. Burke told me, he doubted if you were fit for it: but, now you are in, none of them are sorry. Burke says, that you have so much good humour naturally, it is scarce a virtue.' BOSWELL. 'They were afraid of you, Sir, as it was you who proposed me.' JOHNSON. 'Sir, they knew, that if they refused you, they'd probably never have got in another. I'd have kept them all out.'"

Perhaps the boldest thing Boswell did in the course of his friendship with Johnson was to arrange a meeting between him and John Wilkes. The story of Wilkes belongs to the history-books. Himself a member of parliament, he had in 1763 violently attacked the king and his minister, Lord

Bute, in a famous issue of *The North Briton.* For this he was imprisoned in the Tower and expelled from the House of Commons. But outside Parliament there was much sympathy with him, especially in London, and he quickly became a popular hero. "Wilkes and Liberty for ever" was the cry. He was three times re-elected as member for Middlesex, but each time Parliament refused to let him take his seat. Finally, after being made Lord Mayor of London in 1774, he had a great triumph in the House of Commons in the following year, when all the previous resolutions against him were annulled.

It is not difficult to imagine how Dr Johnson, with his principles of loyalty to king and government, felt towards this hero of popular liberty.

Boswell realised this quite well:

" My desire of being acquainted with celebrated men of every description, had made me, much about the same time, obtain an introduction to Dr Samuel Johnson and to John Wilkes, Esq. Two men more different could perhaps not be selected out of all mankind. They had even attacked one another with some asperity in their writings; yet I lived in habits of friendship with both. I could fully relish the excellence of each....I conceived an irresistible wish, if possible, to bring Dr Johnson and Mr Wilkes together. How to manage it, was a nice and difficult matter."

Boswell went tactfully to work. After getting Johnson's consent to dine at Mr Dilly's, he hinted at strange company:

"'Provided, Sir, I suppose, that the company

which he is to have, is agreeable to you.' JOHN-
SON. 'What do you mean, Sir? What do you take
me for? Do you think I am so ignorant of the
world, as to imagine that I am to prescribe to a
gentleman what company he is to have at his table?'
BOSWELL. 'I beg your pardon, Sir...I should not
be surprized to find Jack Wilkes there.' JOHNSON.
'And if Jack Wilkes *should* be there, what is that
to *me*, Sir?'"

"Upon the much-expected Wednesday, I called
on him about half an hour before dinner, as I
often did when we were to dine out together, to
see that he was ready in time, and to accompany
him. I found him buffeting his books, as upon a
former occasion, covered with dust, and making
no preparation for going abroad. 'How is this, Sir?
(said I.) Don't you recollect that you are to dine
at Mr Dilly's?' JOHNSON. 'Sir, I did not think of
going to Dilly's: it went out of my head. I have
ordered dinner at home with Mrs Williams.' Bos-
WELL. 'But, my dear Sir, you know you were engaged to Mr Dilly, and I told him so. He will
expect you, and will be much disappointed if you
don't come.' JOHNSON. 'You must talk to Mrs
Williams about this.'"

Here, as Boswell says, was a sad dilemma. There
was nothing for it but to approach Mrs Williams.
She was difficult at first, but "gradually softened"
and finally gave her consent that the Doctor
should go.

"I flew back to him, still in dust, and careless
of what should be the event, 'indifferent in his
choice to go or stay'; but as soon as I had

announced to him Mrs Williams' consent,
he roared 'Frank, a clean shirt,' and was very
soon drest. When I had him fairly seated in a
hackney-coach with me, I exulted as much as a
fortune-hunter who has got an heiress into a post-
chaise with him to set out for Gretna-Green.
When we entered Mr Dilly's drawing-room, he
found himself in the midst of a company he
did not know.... 'And who is the gentleman in
lace?'—'Mr Wilkes, Sir.' This information con-
founded him still more; he had some difficulty to
restrain himself, and taking up a book, sat down
upon a window-seat and read, or at least kept his
eye upon it intently for some time, till he composed himself...."

"The cheering sound of 'Dinner is upon the
table,' dissolved his reverie, and we *all* sat down
without any symptom of ill humour.... Mr Wilkes
placed himself next to Dr Johnson, and behaved
to him with so much attention and politeness, that
he gained upon him insensibly. No man eat more
heartily than Johnson, or loved better what was
nice and delicate. Mr Wilkes was very assiduous
in helping him to some fine veal. 'Pray give me
leave, Sir:—It is better here—A little of the
brown—Some fat, Sir—A little of the stuffing—
Some gravy—Let me have the pleasure of giving
you some butter—Allow me to recommend a
squeeze of this orange;—or the lemon, perhaps,
may have more zest.'—'Sir, Sir, I am obliged to
you, Sir,' cried Johnson, bowing, and turning his
head to him...."

The good fare provided by Mr Dilly and the tact

of John Wilkes himself soon made things easier.
Johnson was before long talking in his usual domineering way about poets and players, and eventually he and Wilkes found at least one "bond of union"—a common prejudice against Scotland.
So they "amused themselves with persevering in the old jokes."

"JOHNSON (to Mr Wilkes). 'You must know, Sir, I lately took my friend Boswell and shewed him genuine civilised life in an English provincial town. I turned him loose at Lichfield, my native city, that he might see for once real civility: for you know he lives among savages in Scotland, and among rakes in London.' WILKES. 'Except when he is with grave, sober, decent people like you and me.' JOHNSON (smiling). 'And we ashamed of him.'"

Boswell did not mind this kind of chaff. He was too pleased with his "successful negociation."

Once or twice Johnson went too far, even for Boswell's humble devotion:

"On Saturday, May 2, [1778] I dined with him at Sir Joshua Reynolds's, where there was a very large company...less attention was paid to him than usual, which put him out of humour; and upon some imaginary offence from me, he attacked me with such rudeness, that I was vexed and angry.... I was so much hurt, and had my pride so much roused, that I kept away from him for a week...."

"On Friday, May 8, I dined with him at Mr Langton's. I was reserved and silent, which I suppose he perceived, and might recollect the cause.

After dinner when...we were by ourselves, he drew his chair near to mine, and said, in a tone of conciliating courtesy, 'Well, how have you done?' BOSWELL. 'Sir, you have made me very uneasy by your behaviour to me when we were last at Sir Joshua Reynolds's. You know, my dear Sir, no man has a greater respect and affection for you, or would sooner go to the end of the world to serve you. Now to treat me so——.' He insisted that I had interrupted him, which I assured him was not the case; and proceeded—'But why treat me so before people who neither love you nor me?' JOHNSON. 'Well, I am sorry for it. I'll make it up to you twenty different ways, as you please.' BOSWELL. 'I said to-day to Sir Joshua, when he observed that you *tossed* me sometimes—I don't care how often, or how high he tosses me, when only friends are present, for then I fall upon soft ground: but I do not like falling on stones, which is the case when enemies are present.'"

But these tiffs were rare. "My regard for you" Johnson told Boswell with a sincerity we cannot doubt "is greater almost than I have words to express; but I do not choose to be always repeating it."

He did so, however, in many a letter to his friend:

"My dear Boswell," he wrote "do not neglect to write to me; for your kindness is one of the pleasures of my life, which I should be sorry to lose."

Boswell's reply was no less sincere:

"Be assured, my dear Sir, that my affection and

reverence for you are exalted and steady. I do not believe that a more perfect attachment ever existed in the history of mankind."

David Garrick

EXCEPT for the part he played in Johnson's *Irene*, we have heard little of David Garrick since he came to London in 1737 "with three-halfpence in his pocket."

He at first entered Lincoln's Inn to study the law, but he had a passion for the stage and made his first appearance in the part of a harlequin. Unlike Johnson, he did not have to face a long period of poverty and 'cold obscurity'; he received a legacy of £1000 and before he had spent it all, his acting of the part of *Richard III* in 1741 quickly made him famous.

Mr Pope declared: "That young man never had his equal as an actor and he never will have a rival," and there were "a dozen dukes of a night" at the theatre in Goodman's Fields.

He made large sums of money and in a few years' time became manager of Drury Lane theatre, where he tried hard, but in vain, to make Johnson's tragedy a success.

In the bitterness of his early struggle Johnson was no doubt a little jealous of his old pupil.

"His being outstripped by his pupil" says Boswell "in the race of immediate fame, as well as of fortune, probably made him feel some indignation, as thinking that whatever might be Garrick's merits in his art, the reward was too great when compared with what the most successful efforts of literary labour could attain....His schoolfellow and friend, Dr Taylor, told me a pleasant anecdote of Johnson's triumphing over his pupil David Garrick. When that great actor had played some little time at Goodman's fields, Johnson and Taylor went to see him perform, and afterwards passed the evening at a tavern with him and old Giffard[1]. Johnson...after censuring some mistakes in emphasis which Garrick had committed in the course of that night's acting, said, 'the players, Sir, have got a kind of rant, with which they run on, without any regard to accent or emphasis.' Both Garrick and Giffard were offended at this sarcasm, and endeavoured to refute it; upon which Johnson rejoined, 'Well now, I'll give you something to speak, with which you are little acquainted, and then we shall see how just my observation is. That shall be the criterion. Let me hear you repeat the ninth Commandment, "Thou shalt not bear false witness against thy neighbour."' Both tried at it, said Dr Taylor, and both mistook the emphasis, which should be upon *not* and *false witness*. Johnson put them right, and enjoyed his victory with great glee."

Whether Johnson was right or not may still be argued, but he loved to get Davy back at school

---

[1] The manager of Goodman's Fields theatre.

A Pit check, Goodman's Fields Theatre

Drury Lane Theatre

again. Garrick, too, retained some of his school-
boy tricks of mimicry:

"He could imitate Johnson very exactly....I
recollect his exhibiting him to me one day, as if
saying, 'Davy has some convivial pleasantry about
him, but 'tis a futile fellow;' which he uttered
perfectly with the tone and air of Johnson."

Johnson's provincial accent (he pronounced
once as *woonse*) gave Garrick another opening:

"Garrick sometimes used to take him off,
squeezing a lemon into a punch-bowl, with uncouth gesticulations, looking round the company,
and calling out, 'Who's for *poonsh*?'"

Johnson, for his part, never quite got rid of his
feeling of contempt for the actor's profession. He
often discussed it with Boswell:

"Boswell. 'Sir..., you never will allow merit
to a player.' Johnson. 'Merit, Sir! what merit?
Do you respect a rope-dancer, or a ballad-singer?'
Boswell. 'No, Sir: but we respect a great player,
as a man who can conceive lofty sentiments and
can express them gracefully.' Johnson. 'What,
Sir, a fellow who claps a hump on his back, and
a lump on his leg, and cries "*I am Richard the
Third*?"... Boswell. 'My dear Sir! you may turn
anything into ridicule...a great player does what
very few are capable to do: his art is a very rare
faculty. *Who* can repeat Hamlet's soliloquy, "To
be, or not to be," as Garrick does it?' Johnson.
'Anybody may. Jemmy, there (a boy about eight
years old, who was in the room), will do it as well
in a week.' Boswell. 'No, no, Sir: and as a proof
of the merit of great acting, and of the value which

mankind set upon it, Garrick has got a hundred thousand pounds.' JOHNSON. 'Is getting a hundred thousand pounds a proof of excellence? That has been done by a scoundrel commissary.'"

Poor Bozzy! "I was *sure*, for once," he says, "that I had the best side of the argument." As if that made any difference to Johnson when he was "talking for victory"!

Both Garrick and Johnson were lovers of books —but in a different way. Johnson was "born to grapple with whole libraries," as Boswell's uncle said, but he did not treat a rare volume with the tender care of a collector. When he was putting his books in order, he wore a pair of large gloves "such as hedgers use," and "buffeted" them so that clouds of dust flew round him. When he was reading a new book it was said that "he tore out the heart of it"; when he was tidying his old ones it is to be feared that he sometimes tore off the covers of them. Garrick had some old and valued editions, and seems to have offended Johnson by hesitating to lend them to him. Even Boswell admits that "considering the slovenly and careless manner in which books were treated by Johnson, it could not be expected that scarce and valuable editions should have been lent to him."

Garrick, moreover, had learnt by experience. Here is the story as he told it to Miss Burney:

"'David!' said Johnson, 'will you lend me your *Petrarca*[1]?' 'Y-e-s, Sir!' 'David! you sigh?'

---

[1] The author whom Johnson had first discovered on the apple-shelf at Lichfield. See p. 7.

'Sir—you shall have it certainly.' Accordingly the book, stupendously bound, I sent to him that very evening. But scarcely had he taken it in his hands, when, as Boswell tells me, he poured forth a Greek ejaculation and a couplet or two from Horace, and then in one of those fits of enthusiasm which always seem to require that he should spread his arms aloft, he suddenly pounces my poor *Petrarca* over his head upon the floor. And then, standing for several minutes lost in abstraction, he forgot probably that he had ever seen it."

As his old schoolmaster, Johnson took good care that Garrick should not suffer from swelled head :

"Not very long after the institution of our club, Sir Joshua Reynolds was speaking of it to Garrick. 'I like it much, (said he,) I think I shall be of you.' When Sir Joshua mentioned this to Dr Johnson, he was much displeased with the actor's conceit. *'He'll be of us,* (said Johnson) how does he know we will *permit* him? The first Duke in England has no right to hold such language.' However, when Garrick was regularly proposed some time afterwards, Johnson, though he had taken a momentary offence at his arrogance, warmly and kindly supported him, and he was accordingly elected, was a most agreeable member, and continued to attend our meetings to the time of his death."

Each of them, indeed, was ready to help the other when he could. When the advertisement of Johnson's *Dictionary* appeared in *The Gentleman's Magazine*, there was printed beneath it a compli-

mentary ode, written by Garrick, and ending with
the lines :

> And Johnson, well arm'd like a hero of yore,
> Has beat forty French, and will beat forty more ![1]

When Drury Lane theatre was first opened
under the management of Garrick, the prologue
(one of the two decent prologues in the language,
according to Byron) was written by Johnson. It
is a fine appeal to the public to support Garrick
in ennobling the stage by the revival of Shakespeare :

> Ah! let not censure term our fate our choice,
> The stage but echoes back the public voice ;
> The drama's laws, the drama's patrons give,
> For we that live to please, must please to live.

The truth was, as Sir Joshua Reynolds said :
" Johnson considered Garrick to be as it were
his *property*. He would allow no man either to
blame or to praise Garrick in his presence, without
contradicting him."

Boswell discovered this, as we have seen, at the
famous meeting in Tom Davies's back parlour.

Garrick died in 1779 and was buried with great
pomp in Westminster Abbey. His death provoked
one of the most famous of all Johnson's sen-
tences :

"That stroke of death" he wrote, "has eclipsed
the gaiety of nations."

Of his personal character Johnson said even
finer things and when Boswell tried to press him,
he retired, as usual, defeated :

[1] See p. 28.

DAVID GARRICK

"JOHNSON. 'Garrick was a very good man, the cheerfullest man of his age; a decent liver in a profession which is supposed to give indulgence to licentiousness; and a man who gave away, freely, money acquired by himself. He began the world with a great hunger for money; the son of a half-pay officer, bred in a family, whose study was to make four-pence do as much as others made four-pence halfpenny do. But, when he had got money, he was very liberal....'

[BOSWELL] 'You say, Sir, his death eclipsed the gaiety of nations.' JOHNSON. 'I could not have said more nor less. It is the truth; *eclipsed*, not *extinguished*; and his death *did* eclipse; it was like a storm.' BOSWELL. 'But why nations? Did his gaiety extend farther than his own nation?' JOHNSON. 'Why, Sir, some exaggeration must be allowed. Besides, nations may be said—if we allow the Scotch to be a nation, and to have gaiety,—which they have not. *You* are an exception, though. Come, gentlemen, let us candidly admit that there is one Scotchman who is cheerful.' BEAUCLERK. 'But he is a very unnatural Scotchman.'"

Oliver Goldsmith once wrote a series of playful epitaphs for his friends. These were his first two lines on Garrick:

Here lies David Garrick, describe him who can,
An abridgment of all that was pleasant in man.

Oliver Goldsmith

OLIVER GOLDSMITH, known best to us as the author of *The Vicar of Wakefield*, and described by Boswell as "one of the brightest ornaments of the Johnsonian school" was, like his master, an adventurer in literature.

The son of a poor Irish clergyman, he went, after an unhappy time at school, where he was teased by the boys on account of his disfigurement by small pox, to Trinity College, Dublin.

Here, like Johnson at Oxford, he was a "lounger at the college-gate" and, in spite of his poverty, a leading spirit in college riots, such as the ducking of a bailiff and the gathering of a dancing party "of humblest sort" in his college room.

However, he worked hard enough to get the degree of Bachelor of Arts, and learnt, besides, to write ballads and to play the flute. After three years of idleness he went to Edinburgh to study medicine, the money being provided by a generous uncle. But more of this bounty was spent on fine clothes than on medical books and his restlessness soon drove him abroad to the university of Leyden, where he studied little except in what Johnson calls "the great book of mankind."

With the true spirit of the Irish adventurer he now began his wanderings on foot through Flanders, France, Switzerland and Italy. Sometimes

he had to depend on the tunes of his flute to g
him food and lodging; sometimes he earned a few
shillings "by demanding at Universities to enter
the lists as a disputant." Having thus disputed his
passage through Europe, as Boswell says, he landed
in England at the age of 28 without a shilling in
his pocket.

For him, as for Johnson, there was only one
kind of life possible—the life of "Grub Street."
Here are a few lines from his own *Description of
an Author's Bedchamber* :

The morn was cold, he views with keen desire
The rusty grate unconscious of a fire :
With beer and milk arrears the frieze was scored,
And five crack'd teacups dress'd the chimney board :
A nightcap deck'd his brows instead of bay,
A cap by night—a stocking all the day !

In his early years in London he was, as Boswell
tells us, "employed successively in the capacities
of an usher to an academy, a corrector of the press,
a reviewer, and a writer for a news-paper. He had
sagacity enough to cultivate assiduously the acquaintance of Johnson....To me and many others
it appeared that he studiously copied the manner
of Johnson, though, indeed, upon a smaller scale.
At this time I think he had published nothing
with his name, though it was pretty generally
known that *one Dr Goldsmith* was the authour of
*An Enquiry into the present State of polite Learning
in Europe,* and of *The Citizen of the World,* a series
of letters supposed to be written from London by
a Chinese."

Johnson paid his first visit to Goldsmith in

1761. Dr Percy, a friend of both, gave this account of it:

"The first visit Goldsmith ever received from Johnson was on May 31, 1761, when he gave an invitation to him, and much other company, many of them literary men, to a supper in his lodgings in Wine Office Court, Fleet Street. Percy being intimate with Johnson, was desired to call upon him and take him with him. As they went together the former was much struck with the studied neatness of Johnson's dress. He had on a new suit of clothes, a new wig nicely powdered, and everything about him so perfectly dissimilar from his usual appearance that his companion could not help inquiring the cause of this singular transformation. 'Why, Sir,' said Johnson, 'I hear that Goldsmith, who is a very great sloven, justifies his disregard of cleanliness and decency by quoting my practice, and I am desirous this night to show him a better example.'"

Johnson quickly took Goldsmith to his heart, and praised his writing at a time when the public "*made a point* to know nothing about it."

Goldsmith was an original member of the Literary Club and, rather to Boswell's chagrin, soon became a real intimate of Johnson's household:

"My next meeting with Johnson," says Boswell, "was on Friday the 1st of July, [1763] when he and I and Dr Goldsmith supped together at the Mitre.... Goldsmith's respectful attachment to Johnson was then at its height; for his own literary reputation had not yet distinguished him so much as to excite a vain desire of competition with his

OLIVER GOLDSMITH

great Master. He had increased my admiration of the goodness of Johnson's heart, by incidental remarks in the course of conversation, such as... when I wondered that he was very kind to a man of whom I had heard a very bad character, 'He is now become miserable, and that insures the protection of Johnson....'"

"At this time *Miss* Williams, as she was then called... had so much of his attention, that he every night drank tea with her before he went home, however late it might be...Dr Goldsmith, being a privileged man, went with him this night, strutting away, and calling to me with an air of superiority...'I go to Miss Williams.' I confess, I then envied him this mighty privilege, of which he seemed so proud; but it was not long before I obtained the same mark of distinction[1]."

Goldsmith, indeed, was sometimes rather bitter about Boswell.

"Who *is* this Scotch cur at Johnson's heels?" asked someone. "He is not a cur," answered Goldsmith, "you are too severe. He is only a bur. Tom Davies flung him at Johnson in sport, and he has the faculty of sticking."

The Traveller, published in 1764, at length brought Goldsmith fame, though not a fortune. He received but twenty guineas for it and was still miserable enough to qualify for Johnson's protection.

"I received one morning," so Johnson told Boswell, "a message from poor Goldsmith that he was in great distress, and as it was not in his power to

[1] See p. 46.

R. B. J.

come to me, begging that I would come to him as soon as possible. I sent him a guinea, and promised to come to him directly. I accordingly went as soon as I was drest, and found that his landlady had arrested him for his rent, at which he was in a violent passion. I perceived that he had already changed my guinea, and had got a bottle of Madeira and a glass before him. I put the cork into the bottle, desired he would be calm, and began to talk to him of the means by which he might be extricated. He then told me that he had a novel ready for the press, which he produced to me. I looked into it, and saw its merit; told the landlady I should soon return, and having gone to a bookseller, sold it for sixty pounds. I brought Goldsmith the money, and he discharged his rent, not without rating his landlady in a high tone for having used him so ill."

The novel ready for the press was *The Vicar of Wakefield.*

This is not the place for a full account of Goldsmith's works; but we will glance at one or two.

The picture of English country life in *The Deserted Village* still delights us. Here, for instance, are a few lines on the village schoolmaster:

> There, in his noisy mansion, skill'd to rule,
> The village master taught his little school:
> A man severe he was, and stern to view,
> I knew him well, and every truant knew;
> Well had the boding tremblers learn'd to trace
> The day's disasters in his morning face;
> Full well they laughed with counterfeited glee
> At all his jokes, for many a joke had he.

As a writer of plays, Goldsmith gained a great success with *She Stoops to Conquer.* Johnson, to whom it was dedicated, said:

"I know of no comedy for many years that has so much exhilarated an audience, that has answered so much the great end of comedy—making an audience merry."

Goldsmith wrote histories of England, Greece, and Rome—sometimes inaccurate, but always readable, and, with but a shallow knowledge of natural science, plunged into a work called *A History of the Earth and Animated Nature.* He had, as Boswell says, "a more than common share of that hurry of ideas which we often find in his countrymen."

"Goldsmith told us, that he was now busy in writing a natural history, and...had taken lodgings, at a farmer's house, near to the six milestone, on the Edgeware road, and had carried down his books in two returned post-chaises...I went to visit him at this place...and found curious scraps of descriptions of animals, scrawled upon the wall with a black lead pencil."

When Johnson heard of the project, he said:

"Goldsmith, Sir, will give us a very fine book upon the subject; but if he can distinguish a cow from a horse, that, I believe, may be the extent of his knowledge of natural history."

Goldsmith was certainly not very sound on cows. This is what he says of their horns:

"At three years old the cow sheds its horns, and new ones arise in their place, which continue as long as it lives"1

But all that Goldsmith wrote had charm, and no one was more sensitive to it than Johnson.

In conversation Goldsmith was not so happy. Garrick described him as one

...for shortness call'd Noll,
Who wrote like an angel, but talked like poor Poll,

and Johnson said of him : "No man was more foolish when he had not a pen in his hand, or more wise when he had."

The truth was that Goldsmith's vanity, which made him eager to get in and *shine*, could not bear the rough buffetings of Johnson's talk. "There is no arguing with Johnson," he complained, "for when his pistol misses fire, he knocks you down with the butt end of it."

He was as vain of his fine clothes, when he had money to buy them, as of his literary reputation:

"Well, let me tell you," he said once, "when my tailor brought home my bloom-coloured coat, he said, 'Sir, I have a favour to beg of you. When any body asks you who made your clothes, be pleased to mention John Filby, at the Harrow, in Water-lane.' JOHNSON. 'Why, Sir, that was because he knew the strange colour would attract crowds to gaze at it, and thus they might hear of him, and see how well he could make a coat even of so absurd a colour.'"

Once at a dinner-party Goldsmith became really angry when "beginning to speak, he found himself overpowered by the loud voice of Johnson, who was at the opposite end of the table." When at length he complained, Johnson silenced him by calling him impertinent.

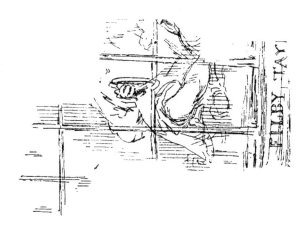

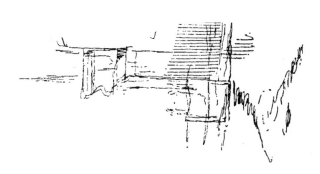

But later, at the Club, they were quickly reconciled:

"'Dr Goldsmith,' said Johnson, 'something passed to-day where you and I dined; I ask your pardon.' Goldsmith answered placidly, 'It must be much from you, Sir, that I take ill.' And so at once the difference was over, and they were on as easy terms as ever, and Goldsmith rattled away as usual."

Sometimes Goldsmith had the last word, as when they were discussing the writing of a good fable, like that of the little fishes:

"'The skill,' said Goldsmith, 'consists in making them talk like little fishes.' While he indulged himself in this fanciful reverie, he observed Johnson shaking his sides, and laughing. Upon which he smartly proceeded, 'Why, Dr Johnson, this is not so easy as you seem to think; for if you were to make little fishes talk, they would talk like WHALES.'"

But these victories and defeats in conversation were only incidents in the history of a well-tried friendship.

When Goldsmith died in 1774 at the age of 46, Johnson wrote to his friend, Bennet Langton:

"Poor Goldsmith is gone...He died of a fever, exasperated, as I believe, by the fear of distress. He had raised money and squandered it, by every artifice of acquisition and folly of expence. But let not his frailties be remembered; he was a very great man."

"Goldsmith" he said many years later, "was a

man who, whatever he wrote, did it better than any other man could do. He deserved a place in Westminster-Abbey, and every year he lived, would have deserved it better."

Westminster Abbey holds a memorial, but not the mortal remains, of Oliver Goldsmith.

For the monument which, at the suggestion of Sir Joshua Reynolds, was set up in the Abbey two years after Goldsmith's death Johnson wrote the inscription.

"I...send you," he wrote to Sir Joshua, "the poor dear Doctor's epitaph. Read it first yourself; and if you then think it right, shew it to the Club. I am, you know, willing to be corrected."

The Club suggested several alterations, the chief of them being that the epitaph should be in English rather than in Latin.

"But the question was, who should have the courage to propose them to him [Johnson]. At last it was hinted, that there could be no way so good as that of a *Round Robin,* as the sailors call it, which they make use of when they enter into a conspiracy, so as not to let it be known who puts his name first or last to the paper....Sir Joshua agreed to carry it to Dr Johnson, who received it with much good humour, and desired Sir Joshua to tell the gentlemen, that he would alter the Epitaph in any manner they pleased, as to the sense of it; but *he would never consent to disgrace the walls of Westminster Abbey with an English inscription.*"

Here we will risk the posthumous wrath of

Johnson and give the first sentence of the epitaph in English:

OLIVER GOLDSMITH
Poet, Naturalist, Historian,
Who scarce left a single kind of writing
Untouched
And touched none that he did not adorn.

Sir Joshua Reynolds

WHETHER we have read Boswell or not, we all know something of the work of Sir Joshua Reynolds. From childhood, almost from babyhood, we are made familiar with *The Infant Samuel* and *The Age of Innocence*.

But it is as a portrait-painter that he is most famous and in the latter half of the eighteenth century there was hardly a single man or woman of note whose portrait was not painted by him. A few of them are reproduced in this book.

Born in Devonshire, Joshua Reynolds came to study art in London in 1741. He was then 18 years old and, except for a year or two spent at Plymouth and two years' study of the old masters at Rome, practically all his work was done, as Johnson's was, in London.

He was the first president of the Royal Academy, founded in 1768, and was made a knight in the same year; he was supreme among the artists of his day as was Garrick among actors and Johnson among men of letters.

He did not have the same hard struggle for fame and fortune as Johnson. At the age of 35, it is true, he was painting portraits for fifteen guineas apiece, but his charm of manner, as well as his skill as a painter, brought him great popularity, and in a few years' time he was making an annual income nearly four times as great as the total sum paid to Johnson for his *Dictionary*.

Reynolds was first attracted to Johnson by one of his earliest prose works—*The Life of Richard Savage*[1].

"Sir Joshua Reynolds told me, that upon his return from Italy, he met with it in Devonshire, knowing nothing of its authour, and began to read it while he was standing with his arm leaning against a chimney-piece. It seized his attention so strongly, that, not being able to lay down the book till he had finished, when he attempted to move, he found his arm totally benumbed."

Shortly after this the two men met for the first time at the house of the Miss Cotterells:

"Mr Reynolds had...conceived a very high admiration of Johnson's powers of writing. His conversation no less delighted him; and he cultivated his acquaintance with the laudable zeal of one who was ambitious of general improvement.... Johnson at once perceived that Reynolds had the habit of thinking for himself...he went home with Reynolds, and supped with him."

[1] See p. 24.

S<small>IR</small> J<small>OSHUA</small> R<small>EYNOLDS</small>

This was the beginning of an "uninterrupted intimacy" to the last hour of Johnson's life.

Johnson took, or pretended to take, no interest in pictures. He is reported to have said once that "he should sit very quietly in a room hung round with the works of the greatest masters, and never feel the slightest disposition to turn them, if their backs were outermost, unless it might be for the sake of telling Sir Joshua that he *had* turned them"!

At another time "Johnson being at dinner at Sir Joshua's in company with many painters, in the course of conversation Richardson's *Treatise on Painting* happened to be mentioned. 'Ah!' said Johnson, 'I remember, when I was at college, I by chance found that book on my stairs. I took it up with me to my chamber, and read it through, and truly I did not think it possible to say so much upon the art.'"

But this was merely playful exaggeration. Johnson was at any rate interested in the portraits of himself, of which Sir Joshua painted several. One of them was set up in Lichfield:

"To Sir Joshua Reynolds, in Leicester-fields

Dear Sir,

When I came to Lichfield, I found that my portrait had been much visited, and much admired. Every man has a lurking wish to appear considerable in his native place; and I was pleased with the dignity conferred by such a testimony of

your regard. Be pleased, therefore, to accept the
thanks of, Sir, your most obliged
And most humble servant,
SAM. JOHNSON.
Ashbourn in Derbyshire,
July 17, 1771.

Compliments to Miss Reynolds."

Mrs Thrale tells another story of one of the
portraits:
"When Reynolds painted his portrait looking
into the slit of his pen and holding it almost close
to his eye, as was his custom, he felt displeased,
and told me he would not be known by posterity
for his *defects* only, let Sir Joshua do his worst. I
said that the picture in the room where we were
talking represented Sir Joshua holding his ear in
his hand to catch the sound. 'He may paint himself as deaf, if he chooses,' replied Johnson, 'but
I will not be *blinking Sam.*'"
Every year Reynolds used to deliver an address
to the Royal Academy. These were collected into
a book with the title *Discourses on Painting* and the
author of them freely owned his debt to Johnson:
"He may be said to have formed my mind, and to
have brushed from it a great deal of rubbish."
"Reynolds" said Edmund Burke "owed much
to the writings and conversation of Johnson; and
nothing shews more the greatness of Sir Joshua's
parts than his taking advantage of both, and making some application of them to his profession,
when Johnson neither understood nor desired to
understand anything of painting."

But Johnson could understand his friend's writing:

"Though he had no taste for painting, he admired much the manner in which Sir Joshua Reynolds treated of his art, in his *Discourses to the Royal Academy.* He observed one day of a passage in them 'I think I might as well have said this myself:' and once when Mr Langton was sitting by him, he read one of them very eagerly, and expressed himself thus :—'Very well, Master Reynolds ; very well, indeed. But it will not be understood.'"

Sir Joshua, as we have seen, was the founder of the Literary Club and was "very constant" in his attendance. Boswell records, too, many a dinner-party where Johnson and he enjoyed good fare and good talk together, but most of the talk recorded is, naturally, Johnson's :

"On Tuesday, April 18, [1775] he and I were engaged to go with Sir Joshua Reynolds to dine with Mr Cambridge, at his beautiful villa on the banks of the Thames, near Twickenham. Dr Johnson's tardiness was such, that Sir Joshua, who had an appointment at Richmond, early in the day, was obliged to go by himself on horseback, leaving his coach to Johnson and me. Johnson was in such good spirits, that every thing seemed to please him as we drove along. Our conversation turned on a variety of subjects. He thought portrait-painting an improper employment for a woman. 'Publick practice of any art (he observed,) and staring in men's faces, is very indelicate in a female'... No sooner had we made our bow to Mr Cambridge, in his library, than Johnson ran eagerly to one side of the room, intent on poring over the backs of the books. Sir Joshua observed, (aside,) 'He runs to the books, as I do to the pictures : but I have the advantage. I can see much more of the pictures than he can of the books.'"

Johnson and Reynolds often rallied each other on the subject of drinking. Reynolds reminded his friend once that he had had eleven cups of tea. "Sir," replied Johnson "I did not count your glasses of wine, why should you number up my cups of tea?"

For long periods of his life, as we have seen, Johnson abstained from wine altogether ; at such times he was liable to be overbearing, not to say rude, in discussing the social benefits of drinking :

"BOSWELL. 'The great difficulty of resisting wine is from benevolence. For instance, a good worthy man asks you to taste his wine, which he has had twenty years in his cellar.' JOHNSON. 'Sir, all this notion about benevolence arises from a man's imagining himself to be of more importance to others, than he really is. They don't care a farthing whether he drinks or not.' SIR JOSHUA REYNOLDS. 'Yes, they do for the time'....I was at this time myself a water-drinker, upon trial, by Johnson's recommendation. JOHNSON. 'Boswell is a bolder combatant than Sir Joshua : he argues for wine without the help of wine ; but Sir Joshua with it.' SIR JOSHUA REYNOLDS. 'But to please one's company is a strong motive.' JOHNSON (who, from drinking only water, supposed every body who drank wine to be elevated,) 'I won't argue any more with you, Sir. You are too far gone.' SIR JOSHUA. 'I should have thought so indeed, Sir, had I made such a speech as you have now done.' JOHNSON (drawing himself in, and, I really thought blushing,). 'Nay, don't be angry. I did not mean to offend you.'"

This is said to be the only known instance of Johnson having blushed. Few, indeed, would have rebuked him so neatly or so gently as the courteous Sir Joshua.

But all Johnson's quarrels with his friends were momentary. In 1782, after Reynolds had been ill, we find him writing:

"Your country has been in danger of losing one of its brightest ornaments, and I of losing one of my oldest and kindest friends: but I hope you will still live long, for the honour of the nation: and that more enjoyment of your elegance, your intelligence, and your benevolence, is still reserved for, dear Sir, your most affectionate, &c.

SAM. JOHNSON."

This is a good example of "Johnsonese" in letter-writing. Nowadays we cannot imagine a letter written in such a style to an intimate friend of 30 years' standing. But Johnson meant every word of it.

On his death-bed his last requests of Sir Joshua were simpler:

"To forgive him thirty pounds which he had borrowed of him; to read the Bible; and never to use his pencil on a Sunday."

Sir Joshua readily acquiesced.

Bennet Langton and Topham Beauclerk

"SIR," said Dr Johnson "I look upon every day to be lost, in which I do not make a new acquaintance," and even Boswell did not attempt "to trace his acquaintance with each particular person."

A task from which Boswell shrank will certainly not be attempted here ; but two friends, who were both original members of the Literary Club and whose names occur very often in Boswell's story, must be considered for a moment—Bennet Langton and Topham Beauclerk.

Bennet Langton, who had come to London "chiefly with the view of endeavouring to be introduced to its [*The Rambler's*] authour," happened to stay in a house visited by Mr Levet, and Mr Levet obtained Johnson's permission to bring his admirer to visit him.

"Mr Langton was exceedingly surprised when the sage first appeared. He had not received the smallest intimation of his figure, dress, or manner. From perusing his writings, he fancied he should see a decent, well-drest, in short, a remarkably decorous philosopher. Instead of which, down from his bedchamber, about noon, came, as newly risen, a huge uncouth figure, with a little dark wig which scarcely covered his head, and his clothes hanging loose about him. But his conversation was so rich, so animated, and so forcible, and his religious and political notions so congenial with those in which Langton had been educated, that he conceived for him that veneration and attachment which he ever preserved. Johnson was not the less ready to love Mr Langton, for his being of a very ancient family."

Langton was "a very tall, meagre, long-visaged man, much resembling a stork standing on one leg"; Johnson, with his usual fondness for nicknames, appropriately called him "Lanky." He visited him at his home in Lincolnshire, at Rochester, and at Warley Camp (where he was stationed with his regiment of militia[1]) and, though he did not always approve of his domestic arrangements ("His table is rather coarse" he said "and he has his children too much about him"), he kept a deep and almost reverent affection for the pious and scholarly country squire.

Not long before his death he was discussing Langton's character with Boswell:

"He said 'I know not who will go to Heaven if Langton does not'....He however charged Mr Langton with what he thought want of judgement upon an interesting occasion. 'When I was ill, (said he) I desired he would tell me sincerely in what he thought my life was faulty. Sir, he brought me a sheet of paper, on which he had written down several texts of Scripture, recommending christian charity. And when I questioned him what

[1] See p. 148.

occasion I had given for such an animadversion, all that he could say amounted to this,—that I sometimes contradicted people in conversation. Now what harm does it do to any man to be contradicted?' BOSWELL. 'I suppose he meant the *manner* of doing it; roughly,—and harshly.' JOHNSON. 'And who is the worse for that?' BOSWELL. 'It hurts people of weak nerves.' JOHNSON. 'I know no such weak-nerved people.' Mr Burke, to whom I related this conference, said, 'It is well, if when a man comes to die, he has nothing heavier upon his conscience than having been a little rough in conversation.' Johnson, at the time when the paper was presented to him, though at first pleased with the attention of his friend, whom he thanked in an earnest manner, soon exclaimed, in a loud and angry tone, 'What is your drift, Sir?' Sir Joshua Reynolds pleasantly observed, that it was a scene for a comedy, to see a penitent get into a violent passion and belabour his confessor."

When Johnson was stricken down by his last illness, "nobody was more attentive to him than Mr Langton, to whom he tenderly said, *Te teneam moriens deficiente manu*"—"When I die, let it be you that my hand holds in its weakening grasp."

Topham Beauclerk, who was at Oxford with Langton, was a man of very different type. He had "the character of being loose, both in his principles and practice"; yet "in a short time, the moral, pious Johnson, and the gay, dissipated Beauclerk, were companions."

"'What a coalition! (said Garrick, when he

heard of this ;): I shall have my old friend to bail out of the Round-house.' But I can bear testimony that it was a very agreeable association. Beauclerk was too polite, and valued learning and wit too much, to offend Johnson...and Johnson delighted in the good qualities of Beauclerk, and hoped to correct the evil. Innumerable were the scenes in which Johnson was amused by these young men."

Here is one of the most entertaining accounts of Johnson in their company :

"One night when Beauclerk and Langton had supped at a tavern in London, and sat till about three in the morning, it came into their heads to go and knock up Johnson, and see if they could prevail on him to join them in a ramble. They rapped violently at the door of his chambers in the Temple, till at last he appeared in his shirt, with his little black wig on the top of his head, instead of a nightcap, and a poker in his hand, imagining, probably, that some ruffians were coming to attack him. When he discovered who they were, and was told their errand, he smiled, and with great good humour agreed to their proposal : 'What, is it you, you dogs! I'll have a frisk with you.' He was soon drest, and they sallied forth together into Covent-Garden, where the greengrocers and fruiterers were beginning to arrange their hampers, just come in from the country. Johnson made some attempts to help them; but the honest gardeners stared so at his figure and manner, and odd interference, that he soon saw his services were not relished. They then repaired to one of the neighbouring taverns, and made a bowl of that liquor called *Bishop,* which Johnson had always liked; while in joyous contempt of sleep, from which he had been roused, he repeated the festive lines,

> Short, O short then be thy reign,
> And give us to the world again!

They did not stay long, but walked down to the Thames, took a boat, and rowed to Billingsgate. Beauclerk and Johnson were so well pleased with their amusement, that they resolved to persevere in dissipation for the rest of the day: but Langton deserted them, being engaged to breakfast with some young Ladies. Johnson scolded him for 'leaving his social friends, to go and sit with a set of wretched *un-idea'd* girls.' Garrick being told of this ramble, said to him smartly, 'I heard of your frolick t'other night. You'll be in the Chronicle.' Upon which Johnson afterwards observed '*He* durst not do such a thing. His *wife* would not *let* him!'"

At another time Beauclerk was tickled by a sudden display of gallantry on Johnson's part:

"When Madame de Boufflers was first in England, (said Beauclerk,) she was desirous to see Johnson. I accordingly went with her to his chambers in the Temple, where she was entertained with his conversation for some time. When our visit was over, she and I left him, and were got into Inner Temple-lane, when all at once I heard a noise like thunder. This was occasioned by Johnson, who it seems, upon a little recollection, had taken it into his head that he ought to have done the honours of his literary residence to a foreign lady of quality, and eager to shew himself a man of gallantry, was hurrying down the stair-case in violent agitation. He overtook us before we reached the Temple-gate, and brushing in between me and Madame de Boufflers, seized her hand, and conducted her to her coach. His dress was a rusty brown morning suit, a pair of old shoes by way of slippers, a little shrivelled wig sticking on the top of his head, and the sleeves of his shirt and the knees of his breeches hanging loose. A considerable crowd of people gathered round, and were not a little struck by this singular appearance."

"Poor dear Beauclerk…" wrote Johnson when he died "His wit and his folly, his acuteness and maliciousness, his merriment and reasoning, are now over. Such another will not often be found among mankind."

Mrs Thrale

FROM what we already know of Johnson, we do not picture him at his ease in ladies' drawing-rooms. But he had violent fits of gallantry, as we have just seen, and he told Boswell once that he considered himself a "very polite man." He could, indeed, be as happy in a boudoir as in a tavern, provided the dinner had been good and his hostess would allow him to have his talk out.

"This year [1765] was distinguished by his being introduced into the family of Mr Thrale, one of the most eminent brewers in England, and Member of Parliament for the borough of Southwark. ..Mr Thrale had married Miss Hesther Lynch Salusbury, of good Welsh extraction, a lady of lively talents, improved by education.... Mr Murphy, who was intimate with Mr Thrale, having spoken very highly of Dr Johnson, he was requested to make them acquainted. This being mentioned to Johnson, he accepted of an invitation to dinner at Thrale's, and was so much pleased with his reception, both by Mr and Mrs Thrale, and they so much pleased with him, that his invitations to their house were more and more frequent, till at last he became one of the family, and an apartment was appropriated to him, both in their house at Southwark, and in their villa at Streatham. Johnson had a very sincere esteem for Mr Thrale, as a man of excellent principles, a good scholar, well skilled in trade, of a sound understanding, and of manners such as presented the character of a plain independent English 'Squire....'I know no man, (said he,) who is more master of his wife and family than Thrale. If he but holds up a finger, he is obeyed. It is a great mistake to suppose that she is above him in literary attainments. She is more flippant; but he has ten times her learning: he is a regular scholar; but her learning is that of a school-boy in one of the lower forms.'... Mr Thrale was tall, well proportioned, and stately. As for *Madam*, or *my Mistress*, by which epithets Johnson used to men-

Mrs Thrale

tion Mrs Thrale, she was short, plump, and brisk. She has herself given us a lively view of the idea which Johnson had of her person, on her appearing before him in a dark-coloured gown; 'You little creatures should never wear those sort of clothes, however; they are unsuitable in every way. What! have not all insects gay colours?' Mr Thrale gave his wife a liberal indulgence, both in the choice of their company, and in the mode of entertaining them. He understood and valued Johnson, without remission, from their first acquaintance to the day of his death. Mrs Thrale was enchanted with Johnson's conversation, for its own sake, and had also a very allowable vanity in appearing to be honoured with the attention of so celebrated a man. Nothing could be more fortunate for Johnson than this connection. He had at Mr Thrale's all the comforts and even luxuries of life; his melancholy was diverted, and his irregular habits lessened by association with an agreeable and well-ordered family. He was treated with the utmost respect and even affection. The vivacity of Mrs Thrale's literary talk roused him to cheerfulness and exertion, even when they were alone. But this was not often the case; for he found here a constant succession of what gave him the highest enjoyment: the society of the learned, the witty, and the eminent in every way, who were assembled in numerous companies, called forth his wonderful powers, and gratified him with admiration, to which no man could be insensible."

Such was the beginning of this friendship, as

told by Bo
Thrale family for some years and could not always

his hero. Mrs Thrale has left us a book of *Anecdotes of Dr Johnson*, and, though Boswell declares
that they are not always accurate, we must quote
a few passages from them to shew how Johnson
used to the full the "comforts and even luxuries"
of a well-furnished home. For he did not trouble
to adapt himself to the household; he made the
household adapt itself to him, "often sitting up
as long as the fire and candles lasted, and much
longer than the patience of the servants sub-
sisted."

"Dr Johnson" says Mrs Thrale "was always
exceeding fond of chemistry; and we made up a
sort of laboratory at Streatham one summer, and
diverted ourselves with drawing essences and col-
ouring liquors. But the danger Mr Thrale found
his friend in one day when I was driven to London,
and he had got the children and servants round
him to see some experiments performed, put an
end to all our entertainment; so well was the
master of the house persuaded, that his short
sight would have been his destruction in a moment, by bringing him close to a fierce and violent
flame. Indeed it was a perpetual miracle that he
did not set himself on fire reading a-bed, as was
his constant custom, when exceedingly unable
even to keep clear of mischief with our best help;
and accordingly the fore-top of all his wigs were
burned by the candle down to the very net-work.
Mr Thrale's valet-de-chambre, for that reason,

kept one always in his own hands, with which he met him at the parlour-door, when the bell had called him down to dinner, and as he went up stairs to sleep in the afternoon, the same man constantly followed him with another....Mr Johnson's amusements were thus reduced to the pleasures of conversation merely....Conversation was all he required to make him happy; and when he would have tea made at two o'clock in the morning, it was only that there might be a certainty of detaining his companions round him. On that principle it was that he preferred winter to summer, when the heat of the weather gave people an excuse to stroll about, and walk for pleasure in the shade, while he wished to sit still on a chair, and chat day after day, till somebody proposed a drive in the coach; and that was the most delicious moment of his life. 'But the carriage must stop sometime (as he said), and the people would come home at last'; so his pleasure was of short duration. I asked him why he doated on a coach so? and received for answer, 'That in the first place, the company was shut in with him *there*; and could not escape, as out of a room: in the next place he heard all that was said in a carriage, where it was my turn to be deaf': and very impatient was he at my occasional difficulty of hearing. On this account he wished to travel all over the world; for the very act of going forward was delightful to him, and he gave himself no concern about accidents, which he said never happened."

Johnson travelled a great deal with the Thrales, visiting Bath, North Wales, Brighton, and even

France in their company[1]. Mr Thrale used to persuade him to mount a horse, as well as ride in a coach:

"He certainly rode on Mr Thrale's old hunter with a good firmness, and though he would follow the hounds fifty miles on end sometimes, would never own himself either tired or amused. 'I have now learned (said he) by hunting, to perceive, that it is no diversion at all, nor ever takes a man out of himself for a moment.'...He was, however, proud to be amongst the sportsmen; and I think no praise ever went so close to his heart, as when Mr Hamilton called out one day upon Brighthelmstone Downs, 'Why Johnson rides as well, for aught I see, as the most illiterate fellow in England.'"

Having settled in her house as one of the family, Johnson did not hesitate to give Mrs Thrale fatherly advice on such domestic subjects as dress, food, and children.

"I advised Mrs Thrale," he told Boswell "who has no card-parties at her house, to give sweetmeats, and such good things, in an evening, as are not commonly given, and she would find company enough come to her; for every body loves to have things which please the palate put in their way, without trouble or preparation."

"Johnson's own notions about eating" says Mrs Thrale "were nothing less than delicate; a leg of pork boiled till it dropped from the bone, a veal-pye with plums and sugar, or the outside cut of a salt buttock of beef, were his favourite dainties."

[1] See p. 141.

MRS THRALE'S BREAKFAST-TABLE

Johnson expressed strong views to Mrs Thrale about children's books:

"'Babies do not want (said he) to hear about babies; they like to be told of giants and castles, and of somewhat which can stretch and stimulate their little minds.' When in answer I would urge the numerous editions and quick sale of *Tommy Prudent* or *Goody Two Shoes*, 'Remember always (said he) that the parents *buy* the books, and that the children never read them.'"

When he suspected her of insincerity, Johnson was as blunt with his hostess as with any of his friends at the club:

" Mrs Thrale, while supping very heartily upon larks, laid down her knife and fork, and abruptly exclaimed, 'O, my dear Mr Johnson, do you know what has happened? The last letters from abroad have brought us an account that our poor cousin's head was taken off by a cannon-ball.' Johnson, who was shocked both at the fact, and her light un-feeling manner of mentioning it, replied 'Madam, it would give *you* very little concern if all your relations were spitted like those larks, and drest for Presto's[1] supper.'"

At another dinner-party on Sunday, April 1, 1781, when Boswell was present,

"Mrs Thrale gave high praise to Mr Dudley Long, (now North). JOHNSON. 'Nay, my dear lady, don't talk so. Mr Long's character is very *short*[2]. It is nothing. He fills a chair. He is a man of

---

[1] Presto was the Thrales' terrier.
[2] Here, as Boswell says, Johnson "condescended" to a pun, a form of wit he generally despised.

genteel appearance, and that is all. I know nobody who blasts by praise as you do: for whenever there is exaggerated praise, every body is set
against a character....By the same principle, your
malice defeats itself; for your censure is too violent. And yet (looking to her with a leering smile)
she is the first woman in the world, could she but
restrain that wicked tongue of hers;—she would
be the only woman, could she but command that
little whirligig.'"

Shortly after this party Mr Thrale died, having
made Johnson one of the executors of his will.

"I could not but be somewhat diverted" says
Boswell "by hearing Johnson talk in a pompous
manner of his new office, and particularly of the
concerns of the brewery, which it was at last resolved should be sold....When the sale...was
going forward, Johnson appeared bustling about,
with an ink-horn and pen in his button-hole, like
an excise-man; and on being asked what he really
considered to be the value of the property which
was to be disposed of, answered, 'We are not here
to sell a parcel of boilers and vats, but the poten-
tiality of growing rich, beyond the dreams of
avarice[1].'"

"The death of Mr Thrale...made a very
material alteration with respect to Johnson's reception in that family. The manly authority of the
husband no longer curbed the lively exuberance
of the lady; and as her vanity had been fully
gratified, by having the Colossus of Literature

---

[1] The brewery is now the property of Messrs Barclay and
Perkins.

attached to her for many years, she gradually became less assiduous to please him."

Johnson, however, continued to spend much of his time with Mrs Thrale both in London and Brighton.

But near the end of Johnson's life there came the final blow to the friendship :

"Dr Johnson had the mortification of being informed by Mrs Thrale, that, 'what she supposed he never believed,' was true ; namely, that she was actually going to marry Signor Piozzi, an Italian musick-master. He endeavoured to prevent it; but in vain."

Though he wrote rather bitterly of the marriage to his friends, Johnson was generous in his farewell letter to Mrs Thrale :

"What you have done, however I may lament it, I have no pretence to resent, as it has not been injurious to me. I therefore breathe out one sigh more of tenderness, perhaps useless, but at least sincere....Whatever I can contribute to your happiness I am very ready to repay, for that kindness which soothed twenty years of a life radically wretched."

Fanny Burney

A FULL account of the twenty years' friend-ship of Johnson and the Thrales would fill a book much larger than this; and in such a volume there would often occur the name of Fanny Burney.

Dr Burney was a musician who had come to London in 1760. He was a member of the Club, and became an intimate friend of Johnson. Frances, who had lived with her father, while her sisters went to school in France, had had a passion for writing since the age of 10, and was eager to meet the great man. She first saw him in 1777 at one of her father's parties, where her sisters were playing a duet. In the midst of their per-formance Dr Johnson was announced.

"He is very ill-favoured..." she wrote to a friend "his body is in continual agitation, *see-sawing* up and down....He is shockingly near-sighted, and did not, till she held out her hand to him, even know Mrs Thrale. He *poked his nose* over the keys of the harpsichord, till the duet was finished, and then my father introduced Hetty to him as an old acquaintance, and he kissed her! When she was a little girl, he had made her a present of *The Idler*. His attention, however, was not to be diverted five minutes from the books, as we were in the

FANNY BURNEY

library; he pored over them, almost touching the backs of them with his eye-lashes, as he read their titles. At last, having fixed upon one, he began, without further ceremony, to read, all the time standing at a distance from the company. We were all very much provoked, as we perfectly languished to hear him talk."

At last Dr Burney dragged him into the conversation, which happened to be about one of Bach's concerts:

"The Doctor...good-naturedly put away his book, and said very drolly, 'And pray, Sir, *who is Bach*? is he a piper?'"

Fanny's greatest achievement was her novel, *Evelina, or a Young Lady's Entrance into the World*. She planned it when she was fifteen and wrote it some years later. She had "an odd inclination" to see her work in print and, without putting any name to the manuscript or letting her secret be known outside her own family, she offered her story to the booksellers and eventually received twenty pounds for it.

When it was published, it took the town by storm. Johnson "got it by heart" and, as soon as the author was revealed, introduced Fanny to the circle at Streatham and made her one of his closest friends. He called her his "dear little Burney" and was always making pretty speeches to her:

"Miss Burney, calling on him the next morning, offered to make his tea. He had given her his own large arm-chair which was too heavy for her to move to the table. 'Sir' quoth she 'I am in the wrong chair.' 'It is so difficult,' cried he with quickness, 'for anything to be wrong that belongs to you, that it can only be I that am in the wrong chair to keep you from the right one.'"

They were guests together of Mrs Thrale at Brighton and one night "to the universal amazement" Johnson went to a ball:

"He said he had found it so dull being quite alone the preceding evening, that he determined upon going with us; 'for,' said he, 'it cannot be worse than being alone.'"

He liked to treat Fanny, his "little character-monger," as a fellow-author:

"A shilling was now wanted for some purpose or other, and none of them happened to have one; I begged that I might lend one. 'Ay, do' said the Doctor 'I will borrow of you; authors are like privateers, always fair game for one another.'"

In his last illness Johnson received Fanny into his house as long as he could. But on 25 November 1784, though his faculties were bright, the machine that contained them was "alarmingly giving away":

"I saw him growing worse, and offered to go, which, for the first time I ever remember, he did not oppose; but most kindly pressing both my hands, 'Be not' he said, in a voice of even tenderness 'be not longer in coming again for my letting you go now.' I assured him I would be the sooner, and was running off, but he called me back in a solemn voice, and in a manner the most energetic, said:—'Remember me in your prayers.'"

Two days before his death, when Dr Burney saw him, his message was the same:

"He was up and very composed. He took his hand very kindly, asked after all his family, and then in particular how Fanny did. 'I hope,' he said 'Fanny did not take it amiss that I did not see her. I was very bad. Tell Fanny to pray for me.'"

On the 20th December, when the "ever-honoured, ever-lamented" Dr Johnson was committed to the earth, Fanny could not keep her eyes dry all day.

The Tour to the Hebrides

"DR JOHNSON" says Boswell at the beginning of his account of this famous tour "had for many years given me hopes that we should go together, and visit the Hebrides."

They had first discussed the project in a coffee-house in the Strand in 1763, Johnson being especially eager to see the patriarchal life of the Highlands—the clansmen living and working and fighting and dying under the fatherly rule of their chieftain. Boswell, knowing something of his friend's love of Fleet Street and of his prejudice against Scotland, "doubted that it would not be possible to prevail on Dr Johnson to relinquish the felicity of a London life."

"To Scotland, however, he ventured," and the faithful Boswell has left us a careful record of his adventures and his talk on each of the 100 days he spent there. This *Journal* was warmly praised by Johnson, who read the manuscript, and was published in the year after his death. Here we must be content with extracts, first following the travellers along the east coast of Scotland, where Johnson found the trees very few:

"On Saturday the fourteenth of August, 1773, late in the evening, I received a note from him, that he was arrived at Boyd's inn, at the head of the Canongate, [Edinburgh]. I went to him directly. He embraced me cordially; and I exulted in the thought, that I now had him actually in Caledonia.... He was to do me the honour to lodge under my roof...."

"Mr Johnson and I walked arm-in-arm up the High-street, to my house in James's court: it was a dusky night: I could not prevent his being assailed by the evening effluvia of Edinburgh.... Walking the streets...at night was pretty perilous, and a good deal odoriferous. The peril is much abated, by the care which the magistrates have taken to enforce the city laws against throwing foul water from the windows; but from the structure of the houses in the old town, which consist of many stories, in each of which a different family lives, and there being no covered sewers, the odour still continues. A zealous Scotsman would have wished Mr Johnson to be without one of his five senses upon this occasion. As we marched slowly along, he grumbled in my ear, 'I smell you in the dark.'"

"WEDNESDAY, AUGUST 18.

On this day we set out from Edinburgh....From

JOHNSON AND BOSWELL ARM-IN-ARM UP THE HIGH STREET

JOHNSON UNDER BOSWELL'S ROOF

an erroneous apprehension of violence, Dr Johnson had provided a pair of pistols, some gunpowder, and a quantity of bullets : but upon being
assured we should run no risk of meeting any rob-
bers, he left his arms and ammunition in an open
drawer of which he gave my wife the charge....
When we came to Leith, I talked with perhaps
too boasting an air, how pretty the Frith of Forth
looked ; as indeed, after the prospect from Con-
stantinople, of which I have been told, and that
from Naples, which I have seen, I believe the view
of that Frith and its environs, from the Castle-
hill of Edinburgh, is the finest prospect in Europe.
'Ay, (said Dr Johnson,) that is the state of the
world. Water is the same every where.'"

Travelling by coach along the coast-road they
visited St Andrews, Dundee, and Montrose and
on Saturday evening reached Aberdeen, where
Johnson was cheered at finding a letter from his
"dear mistress," Mrs Thrale.

"MONDAY, AUGUST 23.
At one o'clock we waited on the magistrates
in the town hall, as they had invited us in order
to present Dr Johnson with the freedom of the
town, which Provost Jopp did with a very good
grace. Dr Johnson was much pleased with this
mark of attention, and received it very politely....
It was striking to hear all of them drinking
'Dr Johnson! Dr Johnson!' in the town-hall of
Aberdeen, and then to see him with his burgess-
ticket, or diploma, in his hat, which he wore as he
walked along the street, according to the usual
custom."

R. B. J.

Johnson wrote of the ceremony to Mrs Thrale:

"I was presented with the freedom of the city, not in a gold box, but in good Latin. Let me pay Scotland one just praise; there was no officer gaping for a fee; this could have been said of no city on the English side of the Tweed."

"TUESDAY, AUGUST 24.

We set out about eight in the morning, and breakfasted at Ellon. The landlady said to me 'Is not this the great Doctor that is going about through the country?' I said, 'Yes.' 'Ay, (said she) we heard of him. I made an errand into the room on purpose to see him. There's something great in his appearance: it is a pleasure to have such a man in one's house; a man who does so much good. If I had thought of it, I would have shewn him a child of mine, who has had a lump on his throat for some time.' 'But, (said I,) he is not a doctor of physick.' 'Is he an oculist?' said the landlord. 'No, (said I,) he is only a very learned man.' LANDLORD. 'They say he is the greatest man in England, except Lord Mansfield.' Dr Johnson was highly entertained with this, and I do think he was pleased too."

After visiting Staines Castle, Banff, Cullen (where Johnson was disgusted by the appearance of dried haddocks with the tea at breakfast), Elgin (where he examined the cathedral "with a most patient attention" in the rain), Fores, Nairn, and Calder Castle, the travellers reached Fort George, at the head of the Caledonian Canal.

"SATURDAY, AUGUST 28.

Mr Ferne and Major Brewse first carried us to wait on Sir Eyre Coote, whose regiment, the 37th, was lying here, and who then commanded the fort. He asked us to dine with him, which we agreed to do. Before dinner we examined the fort. The Major explained the fortification to us, and Mr Ferne gave us an account of the stores. Dr Johnson talked of the proportions of charcoal and saltpetre in making gunpowder, of granulating it, and of giving it a gloss. He made a very good figure upon these topicks....At three the drum beat for dinner. I, for a little while, fancied myself a military man, and it pleased me....

We had a dinner of two complete courses, variety of wines, and the regimental band of musick playing in the square, before the windows, after it. I enjoyed this day much. We were quite easy and cheerful. Dr Johnson said, 'I shall always remember this fort with gratitude.'"

"MONDAY, AUGUST 30.

We might have taken a chaise to Fort Augustus, but, had we not hired horses at Inverness, we should not have found them afterwards: so we resolved to begin here to ride....Dr Johnson rode very well....

When we had advanced a good way by the side of Lochness, I perceived a little hut, with an old-looking woman at the door of it. I thought here might be a scene that would amuse Dr Johnson; so I mentioned it to him. 'Let's go in' said he.... It was a wretched little hovel of earth only....In the middle of the room was a fire of peat, the smoke going out at a hole in the roof. She had a pot upon it, with goat's flesh, boiling....

The woman's name was Fraser; so was her husband's. He was a man of eighty. Mr Fraser of Balnain allows him to live in this hut, and keep sixty goats, for taking care of the woods....They had five children....This contented family had four stacks of barley, twenty-four sheaves in each. They had a few fowls....They lived all the spring without meal, upon milk and curds and whey alone. What they get for their goats, kids, and fowls, maintains them during the rest of the year....

She said she was as happy as any woman in Scotland. She could hardly speak any English except a few detached words. Dr Johnson was pleased at seeing for the first time, such a state of human life. She asked for snuff. It is her luxury, and she uses a great deal. We had none; but gave her sixpence a piece. She then brought out her whiskey bottle. I tasted it."

"TUESDAY, AUGUST 31.

Between twelve and one we set out [from Fort Augustus], and travelled eleven miles, through a wild country, till we came to a house in Glenmorison, called *Anoch*, kept by a M'Queen.... There were two beds in the room, and a woman's gown was hung on a rope to make a curtain of separation between them....We had much hesitation, whether to undress, or lie down with our clothes on. I said at last 'I'll plunge in! There will be less harbour for vermin about me, when I am stripped!' Dr Johnson said, he was like one hesitating whether to go into the cold bath. At last he resolved too....

After we had offered up our private devotions, and had chatted a little from our beds, Dr Johnson said 'God bless us both, for Jesus Christ's sake! Good night!' I pronounced 'Amen.' He fell asleep immediately. I was not so fortunate for a long time. I fancied myself bit by innumerable vermin under the clothes; and that a spider was travelling from the *wainscot* to my mouth. At last I fell into insensibility."

The Island of Skye was reached on September 2, and a few days later came an invitation to cross to Rasay.

"WEDNESDAY, SEPTEMBER 8.

We got into Rasay's *carriage*, which was a good strong open boat made in Norway. The wind had now risen pretty high, and was against us; but we had four stout rowers, particularly a Macleod, a robust black-haired fellow, half naked, and bareheaded, something between a wild Indian and an English tar. Dr Johnson sat high on the stern, like a magnificent Triton. Malcolm sung an Erse song....The boatmen and Mr M'Queen chorused, and all went well....We sailed along the coast of Scalpa, a rugged island, about four miles in length. Dr Johnson proposed that he and I should buy it, and found a good school, and an episcopal church...and have a printing-press, where he would print all the Erse that could be found.

Here I was strongly struck with our long projected scheme of visiting the Hebrides being realized. I called to him, 'We are contending with seas'; which I think were the words of one of his letters to me. 'Not much,' said he; and though the wind made the sea lash considerably upon us, he was not discomposed. After we were out of the shelter of Scalpa, and in the sound between it and Rasay, which extended about a league, the wind made the sea very rough. I did not like it. JOHNSON. 'This now is the Atlantick. If I should tell at a tea table in London, that I have crossed the Atlantick in an open boat, how they'd shudder, and what a fool they'd think me to expose myself to such danger?'...

It was past six o'clock when we arrived. Some excellent brandy was served round immediately, according to the custom of the Highlands, where a dram is generally taken every day....On a sideboard was placed for us...a substantial dinner, and a variety of wines. Then we had coffee and tea....Soon afterwards a fidler appeared, and a little ball began. Rasay himself danced with as much spirit as any man, and Malcolm bounded like a roe....Dr Johnson was so delighted with this scene that he said, 'I know not how we shall get away.'"

"THURSDAY, SEPTEMBER 9.

The day was showery; however, Rasay and I took a walk, and had some cordial conversation.... His family has possessed this island above four hundred years....When we returned, Dr Johnson walked with us to see the old chapel. He was in fine spirits. He said, 'This is truly the patriarchal life: this is what we came to find.'"

This reception of Dr Johnson by Rasay of Rasay may be taken as typical of the hospitality shewn to him by the Highland chiefs, and the story of many another jovial evening, for which there is no space here, must be read in the pages of Boswell's *Journal*.

Besides Skye and Rasay, they visited the islands of Coll, Mull, and Iona; and, on reaching the mainland, returned to Edinburgh by way of Oban, Inverary, Dumbarton, Glasgow, and Auchinleck, the home of Boswell's father.

But before leaving Skye, Johnson had a memorable interview:

"SUNDAY, SEPTEMBER 12.

I was highly pleased to see Dr Johnson safely arrived at Kingsburgh, and received by the hospitable Mr Macdonald....

There was a comfortable parlour with a good fire, and a dram went round. By and by supper was served, at which there appeared the lady of the house, the celebrated Miss Flora Macdonald. She is a little woman, of a genteel appearance, and uncommonly mild and well-bred. To see Dr Samuel Johnson, the great champion of the English Tories, salute Miss Flora Macdonald in the isle of Sky, was a striking sight....Miss Flora Macdonald...told me, she heard upon the main land...that Mr Boswell was coming to Sky, and one Mr Johnson, a young English buck, with him. He was highly entertained with this fancy....I slept in the same room with Dr Johnson. Each had a neat bed, with Tartan curtains, in an upper chamber.

MONDAY, SEPTEMBER 13.

The room where we lay was a celebrated one. Dr Johnson's bed was the very bed in which the grandson of the unfortunate King James the Second lay, on one of the nights after the failure of his rash attempt in 1745–6....To see Dr Samuel Johnson lying in that bed, in the Isle of Sky, in the house of Miss Flora Macdonald, struck me with such a group of ideas as it is not easy for words to describe, as they passed through the mind. He smiled, and said, 'I have had no ambitious thoughts in it.' The room was decorated with a great variety of maps and prints. Among others was Hogarth's print of Wilkes grinning, with a cap of liberty on a pole by him....

At breakfast he said, he would have given a good deal rather than not have lain in that bed. I owned he was the lucky man; and observed, that without doubt it had been contrived between Mrs Macdonald and him. She seemed to acquiesce; adding, 'You know young *bucks* are always favourites of the ladies.' He spoke of Prince Charles being here, and asked Mrs Macdonald, '*Who* was with him? We were told, madam, in England, there was one, Miss Flora Macdonald with him.' She said 'they were very right'; and...very obligingly entertained him with a recital of the particulars which she herself knew of that escape....

Dr Johnson listened to her with placid attention, and said, 'All this should be written down.'"

During his stay in Skye Dr Johnson had a mind to become a chieftain himself:

"THURSDAY, SEPTEMBER 23.

There is a beautiful little island in the Loch of Dunvegan, called *Isa*. M'Leod said, he would give it to Dr Johnson, on condition of his residing on it three months in the year; nay one month. Dr Johnson was highly amused with the fancy. I have seen him please himself with little things, even with mere ideas like the present. He talked a great deal of this island;—how he would build a house there,—how he would fortify it,—how he would have cannon,—how he would plant,—how he would sally out, and *take* the isle of Muck;—and then he laughed with uncommon glee, and could hardly leave off."

On leaving Skye the travellers were driven into Col by a heavy sea. Boswell gives a full account of it and does not try to hide the fact that he was badly frightened. But he endeavoured to compose his mind and sought for something to distract his terror: "As I saw them all busy doing something, I asked Col, with much earnestness, what I could do. He, with a happy readiness, put into my hand a rope, which was fixed to the top of one of the masts, and told me to hold it till he bade me pull. If I had considered the matter, I might have seen that this could not be of the least service; but his object was to keep me out of the way of those who were busy working the vessel, and at the same time to divert my fear, by employing me, and making me think that I was of use. Thus did I stand firm to my post, while the wind and rain beat upon me, always expecting a call to pull my rope....

At last they spied the harbour of Lochiern, and Col cried, 'Thank GOD, we are safe!'"

Johnson lay on one of the beds and "having got free from sickness, was satisfied." This is how he described the voyage to Mrs Thrale:

"After having been detained by storms many days at Sky, we left it, as we thought, with a fair wind; but a violent gust, which Bos had a great mind to call a tempest, forced us into Col."

Boswell was delighted by his friend's sympathy with Highland life:

"SUNDAY, OCTOBER 17.

Dr Johnson here [at Inchkenneth] shewed so much of the spirit of a Highlander, that he won Sir Allan's heart: indeed he has shewn it during the whole of our Tour. One night, in Col, he strutted about the room with a broad sword and target, and made a formidable appearance; and, another night, I took the liberty to put a large blue bonnet on his head."

But to be mistaken for a Scotchman was past a joke:

"THURSDAY, OCTOBER 21.

After a very tedious ride...we arrived, between seven and eight o'clock, at *Moy*, the seat of the Laird of *Lochbuy*....Lochbuy proved to be only a bluff, comely, noisy old gentleman, proud of his hereditary consequence, and a very hearty and hospitable landlord. Lady Lochbuy was sister to Sir Allan M'Lean, but much older....Being told that Dr Johnson did not hear well, Lochbuy bawled out to him, 'Are you of the Johnstons of Glencro, or of Ardnamurchan?' Dr Johnson gave

BOSWELL HOLDING FIRM TO HIS POST

WHIGGISM TERRIBLY BUFFETED

him a significant look, but made no answer; and I told Lochbuy that he was not John*ton*, but John*son*, and that he was an Englishman."

Both Boswell and Johnson found it comfortable to be on the mainland again:

"Saturday, October 23.

We got at night to Inverary, where we found an excellent inn. Even here, Dr Johnson would not change his wet clothes. The prospect of good accommodation cheered us much. We supped well; and after supper, Dr Johnson, whom I had not seen taste any fermented liquor during all our travels, called for a gill of whiskey. 'Come, (said he,) let me know what it is that makes a Scotchman happy!' He drank it all but a drop, which I begged leave to pour into my glass, that I might say we had drunk whisky together. I proposed Mrs Thrale should be our toast. He would not have *her* drunk in whisky, but rather 'some insular lady'; so we drank one the ladies whom we had lately left."

"Thursday, October 28.

On our arrival at the Saracen's Head Inn, at Glasgow...Dr Johnson...enjoyed in imagination the comforts which we could now command, and seemed to be in high glee. I remember, he put a leg up on each side of the grate, and said, with a mock solemnity, by way of soliloquy, but loud enough for me to hear it 'Here am I, an English man, sitting by a *coal* fire.'"

After being entertained by the university professors at Glasgow, the travellers arrived in a few days' time at Auchinleck. Boswell was very nervous about the meeting between his father and Dr Johnson. Lord Auchinleck was a Whig and Presbyterian and commonly referred to Johnson as 'a *Jacobite fellow.*' Johnson promised to avoid awkward subjects of conversation, and all went well for a time; but politics cropped up at length and, to Boswell's distress, "Whiggism and Presbyterianism, Toryism and Episcopacy, were terribly buffeted."

"MONDAY, NOVEMBER 8.

Notwithstanding the altercation that had passed, my father, who had the dignified courtesy of an old Baron, was very civil to Dr Johnson, and politely attended him to the post-chaise, which was to convey us to Edinburgh. Thus they parted. They are now in another, and a higher, state of existence: and as they were both worthy Christian men, I trust they have met in happiness. But I must observe, in justice to my friend's political principles, and my own, that they have met in a place where there is no room for *Whiggism....*

TUESDAY, NOVEMBER 9.

...We arrived this night at Edinburgh, after an absence of eighty-three days. For five weeks together, of the tempestuous season, there had been no account received of us. I cannot express how happy I was on finding myself again at home."

Johnson stayed at Edinburgh for a fortnight and then returned to London "without any incommodity, danger, or weariness."

The expedition to the Hebrides, he said, was the most pleasant journey he ever made.

Lesser Journeys

TWO years after his tour to the Hebrides, Johnson went to France with Mr and Mrs Thrale. It was in the days before, though not long before, the Revolution; and Johnson, who saw Louis XVI and his queen, noted various little points about them—how the king fed himself with his left hand and how the queen, wearing a brown habit, rode 'aside' on a light grey horse.

He saw the sights of Paris and sometimes felt lonely in doing so :

"The sight of palaces, and other great buildings, leaves no very distinct images, unless to those who talk of them. As I entered [the Palais Bourbon], my wife was in my mind : she would have been pleased. Having now nobody to please, I am little pleased."

Besides Paris, which he found "not so fertile of novelty" as the Hebrides, he visited Rouen, Fontainebleau, Versailles, Chantilly, and Compiègne, and admired the cathedrals of Noyon and Cambrai.

People interested him more than places and he summed up a few of his impressions of the French to Boswell :

"The great in France live very magnificently, but the rest very miserably. There is no happy middle state as in England....The French are an indelicate people; they will spit upon any place. At Madame ———'s, a literary lady of rank, the footman took the sugar in his fingers, and threw it into my coffee. I was going to put it aside; but hearing it was made on purpose for me, I e'en tasted Tom's fingers[1]. The same lady would needs make tea *à l'Angloise*. The spout of the tea-pot did not pour freely; she bad the footman blow into it. France is worse than Scotland in everything but climate."

This was Johnson's only foreign tour. Though he often talked of expeditions to other countries of Europe, he was generally content with a post-chaise on an English road and a friend's house or a tavern at the end of it.

On March 19, 1776 he met Boswell at the Somerset coffee-house in the Strand, where they were taken up by the Oxford coach. In his old college his thoughts wandered back to his early days:

"We walked with Dr Adams into the master's garden, and into the common room. JOHNSON. (after a reverie of meditation,) 'Ay! Here I used to play at draughts with Phil. Jones and Fluyder. Jones loved beer, and did not get very forward in the church. Fluyder turned out a scoundrel, a Whig....' BOSWELL. 'Was he a scoundrel, Sir, in any other way than that of being a political scoundrel? Did he cheat at draughts?' JOHNSON. 'Sir, we never played for *money*.'"

[1] It is curious that Johnson, who was not exactly delicate in his manner of eating (see p. 64), should be greatly upset by this. But he complained of the same thing of a waiter in Edinburgh.

"Next morning…we set out in a post-chaise to pursue our ramble. It was a delightful day, and we rode through Blenheim Park….I observed to him, while in the midst of the noble scene around us 'You and I, Sir, have, I think, seen together the extremes of what can be seen in Britain :— the wild rough island of Mull, and Blenheim Park.' We dined at an excellent inn at Chapel-house, where he expatiated on the felicity of England in its taverns and inns….'There is no private house, (said he,) in which people can enjoy themselves so well, as at a capital tavern….The master of the house is anxious to entertain his guests ; the guests are anxious to be agreeable to him : and no man, but a very impudent dog indeed, can as freely command what is in another man's house, as if it were his own. Whereas, at a tavern, there is a general freedom from anxiety. You are sure you are welcome : and the more noise you make, the more trouble you give, the more good things you call for, the welcomer you are. No servants will attend you with the alacrity which waiters do, who are incited by the prospect of an immediate reward in proportion as they please. No, Sir; there is nothing which has yet been contrived by man, by which so much happiness is produced as by a good tavern or inn.' "

"On Friday, March 22, having set out early from Henley, where we had lain the preceding night, we arrived at Birmingham about nine o'clock and, after breakfast, went to call on his old schoolfellow Mr Hector. A very stupid maid, who opened the door, told us, that 'her master was

gone out....' He said to her, 'My name is Johnson; tell him I called. Will you remember the
name?' She answered with rustick simplicity, in
the Warwickshire pronunciation, 'I don't understand you, Sir.'—'Blockhead, (said he,) I'll write.'
I never heard the word *blockhead* applied to a
woman before, though I do not see why it should
not, when there is evident occasion for it. He,
however, made another attempt to make her
understand him, and roared loud in her ear, '*Johnson*,' and then she catched the sound."

However, they met Mr Hector in the street
and Boswell rejoiced to see the two old friends
together. Indeed, he would have liked to prolong
their stay in Birmingham in order to get more
information about Johnson's early life, but Johnson himself was "impatient to reach his native
city."

"We drove on...in the dark, and were long
pensive and silent. When we came within the
focus of the Lichfield lamps, 'Now (said he,) we
are getting out of a state of death.' We put up
at the Three Crowns, not one of the great inns,
but a good old fashioned one, which was...the
very next house to that in which Johnson was
born....We had a comfortable supper, and got
into high spirits. I felt all my Toryism glow in
this old capital of Staffordshire....I indulged in
libations of ale."

At Lichfield Boswell met many old friends of
Johnson—Mrs Lucy Porter, his step-daughter,
Mr Peter Garrick, brother of the actor, Mr Se-
ward, and others. Johnson "expatiated in praise"

of the city and its inhabitants, but it appeared to Boswell that there was "very little business going forward."

" 'Surely, Sir, (said I,) you are an idle set of people.' 'Sir, (said Johnson,) we are a city of philosophers, we work with our heads, and make the boobies of Birmingham work for us with their hands.' "

From Lichfield they set out for Ashbourne, in Derbyshire, the home of another old schoolfellow of Johnson's—the Rev. Dr Taylor.

"There came for us an equipage properly suited to a well-beneficed clergyman;—Dr Taylor's large roomy post-chaise, drawn by four stout plump horses, and driven by two steady jolly postillions, which conveyed us to Ashbourne.... Dr Taylor...was a diligent justice of the peace, and presided over the town of Ashbourne....His size, and figure, and countenance, and manner, were that of a hearty English 'Squire, with the parson super-induced: and I took particular notice of his upper servant, Mr Peters, a decent grave man, in purple clothes, and a large white wig, like the butler or *major domo* of a Bishop."

Boswell wondered at the intimacy between Johnson and Taylor. For Taylor was a Whig and chiefly occupied with country pursuits. His talk was of bullocks and his habits "not sufficiently clerical" to please Johnson. But Johnson, who wrote a good many sermons for him, had hopes of being his heir; and with the memory of his long years of poverty fresh in his mind, he could not neglect such a hope. Quite apart from this,

Johnson never lost his affection for the friends of his youth and it was to Dr Taylor that he first turned after the death of his wife[1]. But neither life-long friendship nor hope of a legacy hindered him from "roaring down" his host.

Thus, on another visit to Ashbourne:

"Dr Taylor's nose happening to bleed, he said, it was because he had omitted to have himself blooded four days after a quarter of a year's interval. Dr Johnson, who was a great dabbler in physick, disapproved much of periodical bleeding....'I do not like to take an emetick, (said Taylor,) for fear of breaking some small vessels.' —'Poh! (said Johnson,) if you have so many things that will break, you had better break your neck at once, and there's an end on't. You will break no small vessels:' (blowing with high derision.)"

Even on the subject of bull-dogs he had the last word:

"Taylor, who praised everything of his own to excess,...expatiated on the excellence of his bull-dog, which, he told us, was 'perfectly well shaped.' Johnson, after examining the animal attentively, thus repressed the vain-glory of our host:—'No, Sir, he is *not* well shaped; for there is not the quick transition from the thickness of the fore-part, to the *tenuity*—the thin part—behind,—which a bull-dog ought to have.'...Taylor said, a small bull-dog was as good as a large one. JOHNSON. 'No, Sir; for, in proportion to his size, he has strength: and your argument would

[1] See p. 45.

prove, that a good bull-dog may be as small as a mouse.'"

Johnson found life rather dull at Ashbourne and often had a day's outing with Boswell:

"After breakfast Dr Johnson and I set out in Dr Taylor's chaise to go to Derby. The day was fine, and we resolved to go by Keddlestone, the seat of Lord Scarsdale....I was struck with the magnificence of the building; and the extensive park, with the finest verdure, covered with deer, and cattle, and sheep, delighted me....'One should think (said I) that the proprietor of all this *must* be happy.'—'Nay, Sir, (said Johnson,) all this excludes but one evil—poverty.'

Lord Scarsdale himself appeared, to do "the honours of the house."

"In his Lordship's dressing-room lay Johnson's small *Dictionary*[1]: he shewed it to me, with some eagerness, saying 'Look'ye! *Quae terra nostri non plena laboris.*' He observed, also, Goldsmith's *Animated Nature*; and said, 'Here's our friend! The poor Doctor would have been happy to hear of this.' In our way, Johnson strongly expressed his love of driving fast in a post-chaise. 'If (said he) I had no duties, and no reference to futurity, I would spend my life in driving briskly in a post-chaise with a pretty woman; but she should be one who could understand me, and would add something to the conversation.'"

In the year following this visit to Ashbourne, 1778, there was fear of invasion. Our army was

---

[1] Johnson produced an abridged edition in 1756.

fully occupied in the war with America and it was thought that France and Spain might seize the opportunity to make an attack upon England. The militia was called out and Bennet Langton was stationed with the Lincolns at Warley Camp. He invited Johnson to visit him there, and Johnson staid about a week, shewing, as he had done at Fort George, a keen interest in military matters:

"He sate, with a patient degree of attention, to observe the proceedings of a regimental court-martial, that happened to be called, in the time of his stay with us; and one night, as late as eleven o'clock, he accompanied the Major of the regiment in going what are styled the *Rounds*, where he might observe the forms of visiting the guards, for the seeing that they and their sentries are ready in their duty....On one occasion, when the regiment were going through their exercise, he went quite close to the men at one of the extremities of it, and watched all their practices attentively; and, when he came away, his remark was, 'The men indeed do load their muskets and fire with wonderful celerity.'"

At the age of 69 he slept in a tent, and enjoyed himself both at the regimental mess and at dinner with the General.

"A camp" he wrote to Mrs Thrale "however familiarly we may speak of it, is one of the great scenes of human life. War and peace divide the business of the world. Camps are the habitations of those who conquer kingdoms, or defend them."

Finally, we must not omit a special journey to
Uttoxeter. Johnson had a long memory, even for
his own failings:

"Once," said he "I refused to attend my father
to Uttoxeter-market. Pride was the source of
that refusal, and the remembrance of it was painful....I desired to atone for this fault; I went to
Uttoxeter in very bad weather, and stood for a
considerable time bareheaded in the rain, on the
spot where my father's stall used to stand. In
contrition I stood, and I hope the penance was
expiatory."

The True-Born Englishman

FOR all his love of a post-chaise, Johnson was
happiest in London. "You yourself, Sir,"
said Boswell when they were in the Hebrides
"have never seen, till now, any thing but your
native island." "JOHNSON. 'But, Sir, by seeing
London, I have seen as much of life as the world
can shew.' BOSWELL. 'You have not seen Pekin.'
JOHNSON. 'What is Pekin? Ten thousand Lon-
doners would *drive* all the people of Pekin : they
would drive them like deer.'"

The town, he said, was his element. He rejoiced in the "animated appearance" of Fleet
Street and "the full tide of life" at Charing Cross,

not so much because he loved shops and pavements better than fields and hedgerows, as because London held his friends, his books, and his amusements. Boswell once suggested that he himself might grow tired of the city if he lived continuously in it:

"JOHNSON. 'Why, Sir, you find no man, at all intellectual, who is willing to leave London. No, Sir, when a man is tired of London, he is tired of life; for there is in London all that life can afford'"; and to the very end he found that "such conversation as London affords, could be found nowhere else."

So, in his last illness in November 1784, he came to London to die. A month later he was buried in Westminster Abbey; Edmund Burke and Bennet Langton helped to bear the pall and Dr Taylor read the service. The monument which was erected in the Abbey was afterwards removed to St Paul's Cathedral, and it is fitting that the nation's memorial of Dr Johnson should be within sound of Fleet Street.

If London meant life to Johnson, it meant the life of England. His prejudice against foreigners was of the old-fashioned kind:

"Like the ancient Greeks and Romans, he allowed himself to look upon all nations but his own as barbarians....If he was particularly prejudiced against the Scots, it was because they were more in his way; because he thought their success in England rather exceeded the due proportion of their real merit....He was indeed, if I may be

FLEET STREET IN JOHNSON'S DAY

allowed the phrase, much of a *John Bull*; much of a blunt *true born Englishman*."

His hatred of the Whigs was life-long and violent—the first Whig, he said, was the Devil; but whatever may be thought of his political opinions, there can be no doubt of his patriotism. What did he mean by a patriot[1]? Here is his definition:

"A PATRIOT is he whose publick conduct is regulated by one single motive, the love of his country; who, as an agent in parliament, has for himself neither hope nor fear, neither kindness nor resentment, but refers everything to the common interest. A true patriot is no lavish promiser; he undertakes not to shorten parliament, to repeal laws....Much less does he make a vague and indefinite promise of obeying the mandates of his constituents....He considers himself as deputed to promote the publick good, and to preserve his constituents, with the rest of his countrymen, not only from being hurt by others, but from hurting themselves."

Johnson had no patience with a popular cry for liberty, such as was raised by the crowds that rallied round John Wilkes. "They make a rout" he said "about *universal* liberty, without considering that all that is to be valued, or indeed can be enjoyed by individuals, is *private* liberty."

Sir Adam Fergusson, a Scotch member of

---

[1] When he made the often-quoted remark 'Patriotism is the last refuge of a scoundrel' Johnson was referring to 'patriots' only in the party sense, to those who made patriotism a "cloak for self-interest."

parliament, once suggested that luxury corrupts a people and destroys the spirit of liberty:

"Johnson. 'Sir, that is all visionary. I would not give half a guinea to live under one form of government rather than another. It is of no moment to the happiness of an individual.'... Sir Adam. 'But, Sir, in the British constitution it is surely of importance to keep up a spirit in the people, so as to preserve a balance against the crown.' Johnson. 'Sir, I perceive you are a vile Whig. Why all this childish jealousy of the power of the crown? The crown has not power enough. When I say that all governments are alike, I consider that in no government power can be abused long. Mankind will not bear it. If a sovereign oppresses his people to a great degree, they will rise and cut off his head.'"

It was his contempt for *political* liberty that made him vehemently support the losing side in the American War. He regarded the colonists as rebels and *Taxation no Tyranny* was the title of a pamphlet he wrote in support of the king's cause.

But what specially enraged him was that the cry of "liberty" should be raised by slave-owners. "How is it" he asked "that we hear the loudest *yelps* for liberty among the drivers of negroes?"

Nearly fifty years before the abolition of slavery was first discussed in Parliament, Johnson had maintained "the natural right of the negroes to liberty and independence." "An individual" he said "may, indeed, forfeit his liberty by a crime;

but he cannot by that crime forfeit the liberty of his children."

Johnson's loyalty to the Crown was strengthened by an interview he had with George III in 1767. It was in the library at the Queen's house[1]:

"His Majesty enquired if he was then writing any thing.... Johnson said, he thought he had already done his part as a writer. 'I should have thought so too, (said the King,) if you had not written so well.'—Johnson observed to me, upon this, that 'No man could have paid a handsomer compliment; and it was fit for a King to pay. It was decisive.' When asked by another friend, at Sir Joshua Reynolds's, whether he made any reply to this high compliment, he answered, 'No, Sir. When the King had said it, it was to be so. It was not for me to bandy civilities with my Sovereign.'"

Had he so chosen, Johnson might have entered Parliament. To the friends of the king, it was urged, he would be found a lamb, to his enemies a lion.

But Johnson knew that he was better fitted to be a public oracle in Fleet Street than to catch the Speaker's eye at Westminster.

A true-born Englishman, he extolled the English virtues of honesty and courage. Of the 'English common soldier' he wrote:

"Our nation may boast, beyond any other people in the world, of a kind of epidemick bravery, diffused equally through all its ranks. We can shew

---

[1] Buckingham House, which stood on the site of the present Buckingham Palace.

a peasantry of heroes, and fill our armies with clowns, whose courage may vie with that of their general."

"Sir," he said at another time "you know courage is reckoned the greatest of all virtues; because, unless a man has that virtue, he has no security for preserving any other."

He himself had no small measure of it. True, he had an "aweful dread of death, or rather 'of something after death,'" but "he feared nothing else, not even what might occasion death":

"One day...when two large dogs were fighting, he went up to them, and beat them till they separated; and at another time, when told of the danger there was that a gun might burst if charged with many balls, he put in six or seven, and fired it off against a wall....He told me himself that one night he was attacked in the street by four men, to whom he would not yield, but kept them all at bay, till the watch came up, and carried both him and them to the round-house. In the play-house at Lichfield, as Mr Garrick informed me, Johnson having for a moment quitted a chair which was placed for him between the side-scenes, a gentleman took possession of it, and when Johnson on his return civilly demanded his seat, rudely refused to give it up; upon which Johnson laid hold of it, and tossed him and the chair into the pit."

Certainly Boswell may be allowed the phrase "much of a *John Bull.*"

Honesty of heart, truth in the inward parts, was with Johnson the one thing needful.

To him no fraud could be innocent; the security of human society depended on truth and was weakened by a man whose words were at variance with his practice.

"Every man" he said (and here John Bull spoke again) "has a right to utter what he thinks truth and every other man has a right to knock him down for it."

To stretch a point in *talking*, in the use of a conventional phrase, did not matter. Common politeness, or the course of argument might demand it. Did he not himself often 'talk for victory'?

What he insisted on was that men should not deceive themselves and others by *thinking* foolishly. "Clear your *mind*" he said "of cant."

"Such," to quote Boswell for the last time, "was SAMUEL JOHNSON." Though he was the foremost man of letters of his generation, it is not for his scholarship or his writings, but rather for his pluck and his patriotism, his humour and his oddities, his blunt common-sense and his large humanity, and, above all, for the expression of these qualities in his talk, that he is best loved and remembered. For to appreciate Johnson's talk one need not be literary; it is enough to be English.

BIBLIOGRAPHICAL NOTE

Boswell's *Journal of a Tour to the Hebrides* was published in 1785 and reached a sixth edition in 1813.

Many of the later editors of Boswell have included the *Tour* in their editions of the *Life*.

It is published as a separate volume in Dent's *Temple Classics*, with a few notes by Arnold Glover (1898) and is contained in a volume of Dent's *Everyman's Library*.

The *Life* appeared in two quarto volumes in 1791 and went through ten editions before the much-criticised edition of J. W. Croker in 1831. The sixth edition, 1811, edited by Malone, is the safest of the early editions. It is not disfigured by the liberties which Croker took with Boswell's text.

Later editions are almost innumerable.

Napier's edition of 1884 included some valuable new material, but the incomparable edition for students is that of George Birkbeck Hill, published by the Oxford University Press in 1887. It is in six volumes, of which four contain the *Life*, one the *Tour*, and one the monumental index to which every student of Johnson must pay his debt of gratitude.

Among modern editions the following may be noted :

Arnold Glover : 6 volumes (text of 1811), annotated. Dent. 1901.

Roger Ingpen : 2 volumes, illustrated. Pitman. 1907.

Among the cheapest and handiest modern reprints are :

The *Oxford* edition. (Two volumes; or, on India paper, in one volume.)

The *Globe* edition. (One volume ; double columns of print. Macmillan.)

The *Everyman* edition. (Two volumes. Dent.)

The contemporary authorities for Johnson's life, other than Boswell, are Sir John Hawkins's *Life*, Mrs Piozzi's *Anecdotes*, Fanny Burney's *Diary*, and anecdotes by many others.

Most of these were collected by the late Dr Birkbeck Hill in his two volumes of *Johnsonian Miscellanies* (Oxford, 1897); two volumes of Johnson's *Letters* were also published by the same editor in 1892.

Of modern criticism on Johnson the following may be recommended:

Lord Macaulay: *Boswell's Life of Johnson.* 1831.

Thomas Carlyle: *Boswell's Life of Johnson.* 1832.

Sir Leslie Stephen: *Samuel Johnson.* (*English Men of Letters* series. Macmillan, 1878.)

G. B. Hill: *Dr Johnson, His Friends and His Critics.* (1878.)

Sir Walter Raleigh: *Six Essays on Johnson.* (Oxford, 1910.)

Lieut.-Col. F. Grant: *Life and Writings of Samuel Johnson*, with a bibliography by J. P. Anderson. (*Great Writers* series. Walter Scott Co.)

Johnson's *Collected Works*, of which there were many editions, e.g. the Oxford edition (*Works*, 9 vols, *Debates*, 2 vols, 1825), are easily obtainable second-hand, as are also *The Lives of the Poets* and *The Rambler*.

The Lives of the Poets and *Rasselas* were edited with notes by Dr Birkbeck Hill for the Oxford University Press.

Johnson's *Poems*, together with the poetry of Goldsmith, Gray, and Collins, are published in a handy form, with introduction and notes by Colonel T. Methuen Ward, in the *Muses' Library* series (Routledge, 1905).

CAMBRIDGE : PRINTED BY
J. B. PEACE, M.A.,
AT THE UNIVERSITY PRESS